THE SIMPLE FACTS

Ozone, a form of oxygen in which there are three atoms in each molecule, occurs naturally in the stratosphere or "ozone layer." This ozone layer protects us from ultraviolet radiation from the sun. Ultraviolet radiation kills living things—it is used as a sterilizing agent in hospitals. There was no life on the land surface of the Earth until the ozone layer developed. Without ozone, there would be no life there now.

Recently, an international scientific study has confirmed that the ozone layer is being destroyed at an ever increasing rate. The hole in the sky is now the size of the United States and the depth of Mount Everest. And, for the first time, the study pinpointed the cause of the ozone's destruction: chemical compounds known as CFCs, which are widely used in everything from propellants in spray cans to the fast-food industry's food cartons to the manufacture of refrigerators and microchips.

John Gribbin, acclaimed science writer and cosmologist, has written *the* definitive book on the ozone layer crisis and its frightening ramifications on our future should we fail to stop the destruction of our sky, our planet, and ourselves.

THE HOLE IN THE SKY

Man's Threat to the Ozone Layer

BANTAM NEW AGE BOOKS

This important imprint includes books in a variety of fields and disciplines and deals with the search for meaning, growth and change. They are books that circumscribe our times and our future.

Ask your bookseller for the books you have missed.

THE HOLE
IN THE SKY

Man's Threat To The Ozone Layer

John Gribbin

BANTAM BOOKS

TORONTO · NEW YORK · LONDON · SYDNEY · AUCKLAND

THE HOLE IN THE SKY

A Bantam Book / May 1988

New Age and the accompanying figure design as well as the statement "the search for meaning, growth and change" are trademarks of Bantam Books, a division of Bantam Doubleday Dell Publishing Group, Inc.

Library of Congress Cataloging-in-Publication Data

Gribbin, John R.
  The hole in the sky.

  Includes index.
   1. Atmospheric ozone—Environmental aspects.
  2. Air—Pollution—Environmental aspects.
  I. Title.
TD885.5.085G75   1988   363.7'392   88-3302
ISBN 0-553-27537-2

Published simultaneously in the United States and Canada

PRINTED IN THE UNITED STATES OF AMERICA

O   0 9 8 7 6 5 4 3 2 1

CONTENTS

PREFACE

On September 16, 1987, the first global treaty aimed at reducing air pollution was agreed at a meeting of representatives of the technologically developed countries held in Montreal, under the auspices of the United Nations. After months of wrangling and disagreements about what and how much should be done, and how soon, an initial twenty-seven nations signed the document, under the terms of which they pledged to reduce the release of chemicals called chlorofluorocarbons, or CFCs, by 50 percent by the end of the twentieth century. The treaty was both welcomed by environmentalists as a positive step and criticized for being "full of holes" and impracticable. Nevertheless, for the first time politicians had taken sufficient heed of the threat to the global environment to take steps aimed at reducing the problem.

The issue that caused this remarkable development was not an event that showed up tangibly in any of the countries that signed the treaty—not acid rain, which destroys forests, or lead pollution from car exhausts, which threatens human health, or any of the other issues that strike close to home. Instead, the politicians, at the urging of the scientific community, were taking steps to protect the ozone layer of the atmosphere, a region many miles above our heads in which a sparse layer of the gas ozone, a triatomic form of oxygen, shields the Earth from incoming solar ultraviolet radiation.

The timing of the Montreal meeting was, in one way, unfortunate. A major part of the reason why the political machinery leading up to the international treaty had been stirred into ponderous motion was the discovery, three years previously, that each spring in the Southern Hemisphere the ozone above Antarctica disappears as the returning Sun brings an end to the long polar night. The depletion of ozone is so pronounced that scientists promptly dubbed it the "hole" in the ozone layer, which the media translated as "the hole in the sky." Following the discovery of the hole, an expedition to Antarctica in 1986 confirmed its extent, and found strong evidence that it was being caused by the presence of chlorine atoms in the stratosphere. The chlorine atoms are themselves produced by the breakdown of chlorofluorocarbons, compounds produced on Earth solely by human industrial activities and widely used as the propellants in aerosol spray cans, to make the bubbles in the foamed plastic cartons used for keeping hamburgers warm, in refrigeration and air-conditioning plants, in the computer chip manufacturing industry, and elsewhere. Even while the politicians in Montreal were debating their response to this human threat to a crucial part of our atmospheric environment, a much bigger expedition, led by NASA and based in Punta Arenas, at the southern tip of Chile, was flying two aircraft through the 1987 ozone hole and was discovering that the effect was more pronounced than ever before. That same expedition also provided the final, incontrovertible evidence—the "smoking gun"—showing that chlorine from chlorofluorocarbons (CFCs) was to blame.

Because the discoveries were so significant, and because of widespread public interest and concern about the threat to the ozone layer, the Punta Arenas team held a press conference at the end of September (just two weeks after the Montreal accord was signed) to let the world know the broad implications of their findings. If, instead, the Montreal meeting had been held two weeks *after* that press conference, instead of two weeks before, it would surely have come up with a much tougher treaty. At an altitude of about 11 miles above the ground, more than half of the ozone above Antarctica was destroyed in the spring of 1987. And changes in the amount of chlorine oxide present marched precisely in step with changes in the amount of ozone. Where chlorine oxide went up, ozone went down, showing clearly that chlorine was destroying the ozone.

Why should we care? Since the 1970s, when ozone was first identified as a key feature of the ecosystem of the Earth, there has been concern about the effects on the ozone layer of high-flying supersonic aircraft (SSTs), such as the Concorde and its (hypothetical) successors. In the mid-1970s, following the SST debate, there was a furious debate in the United States about the damage that CFCs might do to the ozone layer.

The immediate personal threat is that if ozone above our heads is depleted, more ultraviolet radiation from the Sun will reach the ground, causing an increase in the incidence of certain forms of skin cancer in people and possibly damaging crops and animals. One step removed from this threat to human life, atmospheric scientists also warned that changes in the stratosphere could alter the heat balance of the Earth, changing weather patterns and shifting both the wind and rainfall belts that we are accustomed to. A minor feature of the debate in the 1970s, this second threat now looms much larger in the light of recent studies.

Even without any direct measurements to show that the ozone layer was then being damaged, the U.S. legislature took the threat seriously enough to introduce regulations limiting the production and release of CFCs from 1978 onwards. At that time, the United States was producing more than half of all CFCs, and the legislation had an immediate effect in reducing the global emissions of the compounds. The rest of the world, however, ignored the problem, and in the 1980s global emission of these gases was rising once again when the hole in the sky over Antarctica was discovered. With this dramatic evidence of the impact of humankind on the atmosphere before us, it is time to reassess the whole ozone debate, and to decide once and for all, this time on an international basis, whether we really might be better off without chlorofluorocarbons.

The first scientific gathering at which the new results from the Punta Arenas expedition were discussed and set in the context of broader environmental issues was held in Berlin in the first week of November 1987. It was one of a series of workshops that are organized on a regular basis in that city by the Dahlem Konferenzen, to address topics that are of contemporary international interest, timely and interdisciplinary in nature, bringing together many different kinds of scientific specialists. The subject of "The Changing Atmosphere" could not have fitted more closely to this brief. And the scheduling of this particular meeting—to some extent fortuitous, since it was planned months in advance— was as timely as the timing of the Montreal meeting was poor, in relation to the latest observations over Antarctica.

I was fortunate enough to be present at the Berlin meeting, as an invited observer, and it is from that perspective that I am able to bring you an up-to-date guide to the debate and the issues. There is no doubt that there is a hole in the sky over Antarctica each spring, that it is produced as a result of human activities, that it was not there before about 1979, and that it was "deeper" (in the sense that more ozone had been removed) in 1987 than ever before. Why we should care about this, what the implications are for the future, and the steps we should take, both as individuals and as a global community, to minimize any threats to life on Earth are the subject matter of this book. I could not have written it without the opportunity to attend the Dahlem workshop, and I am grateful to Silke Bernhard and her team for the invitation to attend, and for organizing such a well-timed and well-organized gathering. Most of all, though, I would like to thank the eleven members of the group at that meeting who specifically discussed changes in Antarctic ozone. Although some of them seemed alarmed at first to find a journalist sitting in on those discussions, no punches were pulled in the debate, and they all found time to provide me with information about their own work on the problem. They were: Guy Brasseur, of the U.S. National Center for Atmospheric Research; Joe Farman, of the British Antarctic Survey; Ivar Isaksen, of the University of Oslo; Bernd Krüger of the Alfred Wegener Institute in Bremerhaven; Karin Labitzke, of the Free University of Berlin; Jerry Mahlman, of Princeton University; Pat McCormick, of the NASA-Langley Research Center; Phil Solomon, of the State University of New York; Richard Stolarski, of NASA-Goddard; Richard Turco, of R&D Associates; and Bob Watson, of NASA, Washington.

Other members of the workshop, involved primarily in other aspects of the discussions on the changing atmosphere, also found time to correct some of my misapprehensions. Thanks to: Bob Charlson, of the University of Washington at Seattle; Ralph Cicerone, of NCAR (National Center for Atmospheric Research); Paul Crutzen, of the Max Planck Institute for Chemistry; Jim Lovelock, from Coombe Mill; and Sherry

Rowland, of the University of California at Irvine. Any remaining misconceptions are entirely my own fault.

John Gribbin
December 7, 1987

CHAPTER ONE

OXYGEN, OZONE AND LIFE

Ozone is a pale blue gas that is poisonous to human life even in small concentrations. It is produced by electric discharges—naturally by lightning, and artificially by high voltage electrical equipment—and has a characteristic pungent odor. It can also arise near ground level through the effects of chemical reactions involving sunlight acting on pollution; ozone at ground level forms part of photochemical smog. Close up, there is little to be said in favor of ozone, although it does have its uses in the chemical industry, as a bleaching agent, and as a strong germicide used to sterilize both drinking water and swimming pools. But at a safe distance, ozone is essential to our well-being. The ozone in the stratosphere above our heads protects the surface of the Earth from ultraviolet radiation produced by the Sun, which might otherwise sweep away life from most of the land on our planet. And ozone is a form of oxygen, the active ingredient of the air that we breathe, the gas that is essential for all forms of animal life on Earth.

The difference is simply that molecules of ordinary oxygen each contain two atoms, while molecules of ozone contain three; that is enough to make the difference between life and death, for any animal that breathed in more than a trace of ozone; but ozone has also been intimately connected with the emergence of life on Earth.

The atmosphere of the Earth today is a warm blanket, rich in oxygen, that helps to maintain conditions suitable for life as we know it. That is hardly surprising, since life as we know it has evolved to fit the conditions found under that blanket of air. Part of the concern caused by the discovery of a hole in the sky over Antarctica, however, is that the atmosphere may now be changing, so that conditions never experienced by our kind of life could become common on Earth.

For convenience, atmospheric scientists divide up the atmosphere, notionally, into layers. These layers are most simply described in terms of the way temperature changes with altitude, but the boundaries between them are never as sharp as the labels assigned by the scientists might imply. In reality, the boundaries between layers are always more or less indistinct, with gases mixing upward and downward across the boundaries.

Air close to the ground is warm, because the ground itself (and the surface of the sea) is warm. Sunlight passing through the atmosphere does not heat it directly (at least, not near the ground), but is absorbed by the sea, by the land, or by vegetation on the land. The warm surface of the Earth then radiates heat back out toward space; but this outward flow of radiation is at much longer wavelengths than sunlight, in the infrared part of the spectrum. Infrared radiation on its way out *is* partly absorbed by the atmosphere near the ground, and makes it warm. The process is known, for obvious reasons, as the greenhouse effect. The warming falls off with height—the farther away from the warm surface of the Earth, the colder it gets—up to an altitude of about 7 miles, where the temperature is roughly −75 degrees F. This "about" is a particularly vague average, which conceals the fact that the cooling stops at about 5 miles above the poles, but as high as 10 miles over the equator. The layer of the atmosphere below this boundary is called the troposphere. The boundary itself is called the tropopause and marks the beginning of a layer in which the temperature first holds steady with increasing altitude, then begins to increase with increasing altitude.

Up to about 30 miles, temperature increases with altitude, until at that height above the ground the air, although very thin, is nearly as warm as the air at sea level. This layer of the atmosphere, from a little below 10 miles up to 30 miles, is the stratosphere, and the boundary at the top of the stratosphere, where it is warmest, is called the stratopause. Once again, however, global averages conceal important regional variations. Although on average the coldest part of the stratosphere is at about −75 degrees F, over the polar regions in winter, when the Sun never rises, it can get much colder than this, with important consequences for the ozone layer.

Above the stratopause, the atmosphere cools once again through the mesosphere, to an altitude of about 50 miles, then warms again in the thermosphere, where there are so few molecules about that the concept of temperature has long since lost its everyday meaning. These layers above the stratopause, however, play very little part in the story of ozone and the hole in the sky.

The lowest layer of the atmosphere, the troposphere, is the part that we breath and the part in which weather, driven by convection ("hot air rises"), occurs. Although the layer is relatively thin, because air at the ground is squashed by the weight of the air above it, the troposphere is the densest part of the atmosphere and contains 85 percent of the atmosphere's mass. The

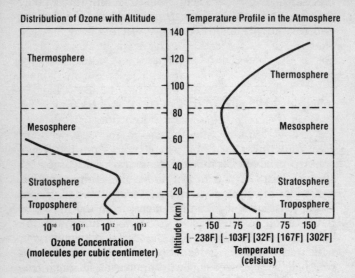

Distribution of Ozone with Altitude

Thermosphere

Mesosphere

Stratosphere

Troposphere

10^{10} 10^{11} 10^{12} 10^{13}

Ozone Concentration
(molecules per cubic centimeter)

Temperature Profile in the Atmosphere

Thermosphere

Mesosphere

Stratosphere

Troposphere

Altitude (km)

140 — 120 — 100 — 80 — 60 — 40 — 20

−150   −75   0   75   150
[−238F] [−103F] [32F] [167F] [302F]

Temperature
(celsius)

stratosphere contains virtually all of the remaining 15 percent—the mass of the air below about 25 miles altitude is more than 99 percent of the total mass of the atmosphere. The air in the stratosphere is "thin" in the other sense of the word, highly rarified compared with air at ground level.

But, unlike the troposphere, and in spite of its low density, the stratosphere absorbs heat from the Sun, in the form of ultraviolet radiation. It does so because oxygen seeping up from the troposphere below absorbs energy from the Sun. The solar radiation breaks apart the two atoms of oxygen in a molecule leaving each one free to link up with another molecule of diatomic oxygen, and forming two molecules of ozone as a result. So the term "ozone layer" is synonymous with "stratosphere." Because the stratosphere is warmer at higher altitudes, hot air no longer rises there, since the air above is hotter than the air below, and convection cannot occur. So, in a very real sense, the stratosphere acts as a lid on the troposphere, keeping convection, and weather, below the tropopause.

THE OZONE LAYER TODAY

The ozone layer exists because oxygen from the troposphere, produced by living things, seeps up into the stratosphere and reacts with sunlight to form triatomic molecules of ozone. Averaging over all altitudes, the air today contains about 75 percent nitrogen (by mass), 23 percent oxygen (almost all in the familiar diatomic form), 0.05 percent carbon dioxide, and 1.28 percent argon, with traces of other gases. It wasn't always like this, as we shall see. However, the presence of so much free oxygen today explains how the ozone layer is maintained.

The explanation depends on the nature of the radiation emitted by the Sun, and on the way in which both ozone and oxygen (whenever I use the term *oxygen* without qualification I mean the diatomic form) respond to that radiation. Most of the energy of the Sun is emitted in the form of yellow light, which has wavelengths in the range from about 500 to 600 nanometers (nm; 1 nm is one-billionth of a meter, 10^{-9} m—a meter is 3.28 feet). The range of light visible to our eyes is from red, at 76 nm, to violet, at 400 nm, but there is still a significant amount of solar energy radiated either side of this band, in the infrared and the ultraviolet (UV). It is the ultraviolet end of the spectrum that plays a part in maintaining the stratosphere.

All molecules respond to specific wavelengths of radiation. A particular amount of energy is needed to break apart any particular molecular bond, such as the one between the two atoms in a molecule of oxygen.

Electromagnetic radiation, such as the light from the Sun, can be thought of in terms of packets of energy, called photons. Energy packets with shorter wavelengths (higher frequency) contain more energy than those with longer wavelengths (lower frequency). The energy emitted by the Sun in the ultraviolet part of the spectrum is weak compared with the energy emitted in the yellow band, in the sense that there are fewer energy packets emitted with ultraviolet wavelengths. But each of those ultraviolet energy packets packs more of a punch than a single energy packet of yellow light. Oxygen molecules respond particularly strongly to wavelengths below 190 nm, in the ultraviolet band. Energy packets with those wavelengths break the bond between the two atoms in an oxygen molecule, because each energy packet carries more energy than the bond holding the atoms together. The resulting reaction, called photodissociation, can be represented schematically by an equation:

$$O_2 + UV \rightarrow O + O$$

In the next stage of the ozone-formation process, another molecule has to be present to act as a catalyst. This molecule is usually nitrogen, the most common constituent of the atmosphere, but it could be almost anything, so we can label it M:

$$O + O_2 + M \rightarrow O_3 + M$$

The reaction that produces ozone gives up energy to the extra molecule M, which moves faster as a result. When molecules of a gas move faster, that means the gas is hotter. So the effect of solar ultraviolet with wavelengths below 190 nm on oxygen molecules in the stratosphere is to create ozone and to warm the stratosphere. Most of the solar UV with wavelengths shorter than 200 nm is absorbed in this way, and some of the radiation with wavelengths up to about 240 nm. But ozone does not continue to build up in the atmosphere, even above the tropopause, because ozone molecules themselves interact both with sunlight and with other chemicals, being broken apart and, ultimately, reforming molecules of oxygen.

The amount of energy being absorbed in a particular region of the stratosphere depends on how many oxygen molecules are around to intercept the ultraviolet radiation, as well as on the strength of the radiation itself. There are more oxygen atoms lower in the stratosphere, where the air is denser and closer to the troposphere, where the oxygen comes from. But the ultraviolet radiation is strongest at the top of the atmosphere, before any of it has been absorbed. In addition, in order to make ozone an oxygen atom produced by the breakup of an oxygen molecule has to find a partner, in the form of another oxygen molecule, and, once again, this is easier where the air is more dense. So there is a tradeoff, which results in the greatest concentration of ozone somewhere in the middle of the stratosphere, between about 12 and 20 miles altitude.

Once ozone forms, it is broken apart more easily than is oxygen. The binding energy that holds the molecule together is less than the binding energy of oxygen, and it is relatively easy for an energy packet with longer wavelength, but still in the ultraviolet part of the spectrum, to knock one oxygen atom out of a molecule of ozone. This longer-wavelength ultraviolet, slightly nearer to the peak of the Sun's energy output, is more abundant than the higher-energy UV, which breaks up oxygen molecules. The odds are stacked heavily against ozone, and the only reason why it exists in the atmosphere at all is because there is so much oxygen around, providing the opportunity for many of the interactions that make ozone to take place. Virtually all of the radiation with wavelengths between 230 and 290 nm that enters our atmosphere is absorbed by ozone in the stratosphere and never reaches the troposphere, let alone the ground; some of the radiation with wavelengths up to 350 nm is also absorbed. The process is very similar to the way oxygen is broken up by more energetic UV:

$$O_3 + UV \rightarrow O + O_2$$

Most of the single oxygen atoms produced in this way quickly meet up with another oxygen *molecule* and reform molecules of ozone. There has been little effect on the *chemistry* of the stratosphere—but remember that there *has* been an overall absorption of solar energy, making the stratosphere warmer. But there are other reactions going on as well, which do convert the ozone back into oxygen. Free atoms of oxygen produced by the interaction with ultraviolet may simply meet another ozone molecule, with the result:

$$O + O_3 \rightarrow O_2 + O_2$$

and there is a whole family of chemical reactions of the kind

$$NO + O_3 \rightarrow NO_2 + O_2$$
$$NO_2 + O \rightarrow NO + O_2$$

which do the same job with the aid of a catalyst (in this case one of the oxides of nitrogen, NO), which is returned to the atmosphere at the end of the reaction. This is important, because in such a process one molecule of NO can go round and round the cycle many times, "scavenging" ozone from the air and converting it into oxygen, while staying unchanged itself. An equivalent pair of reactions with chlorine (Cl) in place of the NO would be very effective at scavenging ozone; but chlorine is rare in the stratosphere—or rather, it was, until we started releasing CFCs. Calculating how much this human influence may affect the natural balance is, however, no easy task.

Even though complex molecules are broken down by solar ultraviolet in the stratosphere, which simplifies the picture considerably, the chemists who try to work out details of the overall ozone budget, balancing the losses by these kinds of processes against the gains by photodissociation of oxygen, have to work with calculations of interactions involving 50 or more chemical compounds, 50 or more associated photodissociation processes, and maybe 150 chains of chemical reactions. Hardly surprisingly, they cannot predict precisely what the effect of disturbing the natural system—for example, by adding a certain amount of chlorine—will be. For now, I will concentrate on the broad picture of the natural state of the ozone layer, which contains enough surprises to suggest that it is a miracle the chemists can tell us anything about what might happen if it were disturbed.

If the stratosphere is disturbed, it takes some time for the chemical system to return to its equilibrium (or to set up a new equilibrium) with the income and expenditure of ozone in balance. But the time this takes itself depends on the altitude in the stratosphere. Above about 25 miles, it may take only a few minutes for equilibrium to be reasserted, while below about 19 miles altitude it can take several days. Since the reactions involved depend on the presence of sunlight, and must follow (or try to follow) the cycle of day and night, this means that the lower part of the stratosphere, constantly disturbed by interactions with the troposphere and influxes of fresh oxygen, is never really in equilibrium at all. This feature of the ozone layer is dramatically illustrated by observations, looking up through the atmosphere, which show that the concentration of ozone above our heads actually increases at night, when there are no solar ultraviolet energy packets around to drive the reactions.

These concentrations are measured by spectroscopy, analyzing the light from stars or the Moon, or the Sun itself, and picking out the dark lines in the spectrum caused by absorption in the ozone layer. The strength of those lines reveals the concentration of ozone in a column above our heads, and shows the nighttime increase. This is probably because at altitudes above about 25 miles, where the atmosphere responds quickly to changes, the overall balance of the reactions destroys

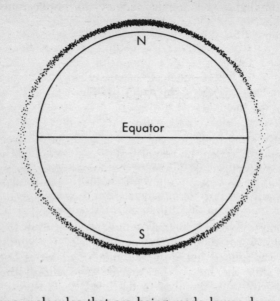

ozone molecules that are being made lower down and filtering up to this height. At night, this destruction stops within a few minutes. Lower down, however, where the balance of the reactions is producing ozone, by the time the atmosphere begins to "notice" that the Sun has set, it is already coming up again. All through the night, single oxygen atoms produced by photodissociation the preceding day are meeting up with oxygen molecules and forming new molecules of ozone.

Ozone is constantly being produced, and constantly being destroyed in the stratosphere, by interactions involving sunlight and oxygen. It is a mistake to think of it as a finite resource, like oil, that can be destroyed once and for all, or like a soap bubble that, once pricked, is gone forever. What could happen is that the balance of the set of equilibrium reactions that maintain the layer may be shifted, in favor of either less ozone or more. The story of the emergence of life on

Earth highlights just how far ranging the implications might be.

OXYGEN AND LIFE

The early atmosphere of our planet contained no free oxygen at all. When the planet first formed, from many smaller objects such as asteroids and meteorites, which were pulled together by gravity and fused into one large lump in orbit around the young Sun, it had no atmosphere at all, and can have gained a blanket of gases only by volcanic activity and outgassing from the hot rocks. Formed by collisions and impacts, the young planet was indeed hot, just as a meteor crater is hot shortly after the meteor has arrived, and almost the whole surface was involved in the initial volcanic outpourings. As the Earth cooled at the surface and shrank inward a little under the pull of gravity, gravitational energy was released in its interior, adding to the energy produced by naturally occurring radioactive elements, and keeping the interior hot and molten. Natural radioactivity keeps the interior of the Earth molten even today, more than four thousand million years later. Throughout the past 4.5 billion years, since the Solar System formed, volcanoes, geysers, and similar forms of activity have been pouring out gases, albeit in diminishing quantities as the Earth has aged. What were those gases, and where have they all gone?

The simple answer is that a large proportion was water, and it went to form the oceans of the Earth. Figures given by various experts studying different volcanoes vary slightly, but by and large volcanic gases today are a mixture chiefly of water vapor (about 80 percent) and carbon dioxide (about 12 percent), with significant amounts of sulfur dioxide (7 percent), a smidgen of nitrogen (1 percent), and traces of compounds containing related substances, such as hydrogen sulfide, ammonia, and methane. There is no reason to think that the gases produced by outgassing early in the history of the Earth were substantially different from this mixture, and good evidence that they were much the same. Although many textbooks still teach that the early atmosphere of our planet was dominated by methane and ammonia, this is now generally regarded as a bad guess, based on inappropriate comparisons with Jupiter, Saturn, Uranus, and Neptune, the giant planets of the Solar System.

Those planets are far from the Sun, huge, and nothing like the Earth. The two planets that do resemble the Earth, in some ways, are our nearest neighbors, Venus (almost the same size as Earth but closer to the Sun) and Mars (smaller than Earth and farther from the Sun). Both those planets have atmospheres rich in carbon dioxide. Venus has a superthick blanket that traps heat very efficiently and has sent temperatures soaring far above the boiling point of water, while Mars has a tenuous layer, with a weak greenhouse effect that has not been able to prevent the planet from freezing. Earth, with a nitrogen-oxygen atmosphere, seems to be the odd one out; but that can now be understood as a result of the presence of our oceans of water, and the relative distances of the three planets from the Sun.

Venus was always too hot for oceans to form, and Mars, although it may once have had oceans of liquid water on its surface, is now too cold. It has frozen both because it is farther from the Sun than we are and because, being smaller than Earth, its gravity has been too weak to hold on to a significant blanket of air to trap infrared radiation. Earth was, and is, in the right place, at the right distance from the Sun, for the water that makes up the bulk of volcanic gases to form liquid oceans, and those liquid oceans have very efficiently taken up carbon dioxide, dissolving it out of the air and laying it down as sediments rich in carbonates, such as limestone.

Water was also the key to the origin of life on Earth. Although there is evidence that single-celled forms of life were around in the oceans well within a billion years of the formation of the planet, multicelled life forms appeared only about 600 million years ago, almost four billion years after the Earth formed, and plant life emerged onto dry land only about 420 million years ago.* The reason for the delay is most probably that it took that long to change the atmosphere into something resembling its present composition. Oxygen could have been released in the early atmosphere as soon as the atmosphere formed, by photodissociation of water vapor caused by ultraviolet radiation from the Sun, breaking hydrogen and oxygen apart just as oxygen molecules are broken apart in the stratosphere today. But calculations show that this process could never produce more than one-thousandth of the oxygen in the air today. The inescapable conclusion is that the oxygen in the air was produced by the action of living things. Plants converted large amounts of the available carbon dioxide, the fraction that had not dissolved in the seas, into carbon and oxygen, by photosynthesis. But where did the living things that did the job come from?

Until the atmosphere developed a significant proportion of oxygen, solar UV reached down to the ground, sterilizing the surface of the Earth. Nobody knows exactly how life emerged, but all the evidence suggests that ultraviolet radiation may have been an important contributor, providing the energy to rearrange molecules and stimulate chemical processes in pools of water on the surface of the young planet—pools graphically

---

*The evidence for these sweeping assertions can be found in my book *Genesis* (See bibliography, p. 183).

referred to as "primordial soup." Too much ultraviolet, of course, would have been a bad thing, destroying complex molecules faster than they could be built up. Had there been no UV at all, the chemical reactions might not have proceeded as required. Somewhere, the balance must have been just right. One intriguing suggestion is that the right conditions occurred only where about 30 feet of water were available to screen out the worst of the ultraviolet, so that the ponds in which the primordial soup brewed may have been about that deep. But whatever the details—and they are unlikely ever to be known for sure—the fact is that life did get a grip in the waters of the Earth and soon began to modify its environment.

For the earliest forms of life on Earth, oxygen was a poison. The gas reacts vigorously with other substances, especially the kinds of substances that are important to life—compounds containing hydrogen and carbon. But the gas was inevitably produced when living organisms began to break down carbon dioxide molecules, using the energy from sunlight, and to use the carbon in the construction of their own cells. The very first organisms simply fed off the chemical riches of the primordial soup, the complex molecules built up with the aid of ultraviolet energy. This life process is called fermentation; it continues today where organisms such as yeasts can get access to food molecules, such as sugar, which have been built up somewhere else. But as the supply of chemical soup began to be used up, there was an evolutionary pressure on the original organisms to find other sources of energy. Their response was to develop photosynthesis, taking sunlight in the visible part of the spectrum, where the Sun is brightest even though each energy packet is not as powerful as the energy packets in the ultraviolet, and using it to build up the molecules they needed.

Some of those early life forms locked up the dangerously reactive oxygen produced by photosynthesis in other compounds. But that added a complication to the life process, a complication that set them at a disadvantage compared with organisms that simply released a dribble of oxygen into the sea as a waste product. The analogy between this kind of behavior and the attitude of some human beings to our pollution of the present environment is too obvious to labor, but adds a nice touch of irony to the story. At first, the small amount of oxygen being released had only a modest impact on the environment. It reacted with other substances and was bound up in oxidized surface rocks. Photosynthesis was "invented" about 2.7 billion years ago, and huge deposits of iron oxides—rusty "red beds"—are found in geological formations about 2.6 billion years old. But there was a limit to how much oxygen the environment could absorb, and it began to build up inexorably in the atmosphere. Organisms that could not shield themselves from its reactive properties—including organisms that were themselves oxygen emitters—were simply poisoned and died out. However, others flourished. And once the concentration of oxygen in the air reached about 1 percent, it became possible for life to develop a new trick—respiration.

In fermentation, living things simply feed off chemical riches that have been provided by other means. Whether by the action of ultraviolet light on the primordial soup, or by photosynthesis carried out by other organisms, they neither know nor care. In photosynthesis, living things use energy from the Sun directly and discard oxygen as a waste product. And in respiration, living things use the energy available from letting oxygen react with carbon as their power supply, releasing carbon dioxide back into the environment. Respiration involves a slow form of burning, and it provides more energy, more quickly, than photosynthesis—which is why you don't see a tree running about. But life forms like us, which rely on respiration, could evolve only when life forms that use photosynthesis had begun the work of changing the Earth's atmosphere from one rich in carbon dioxide into one rich in oxygen. (We also, of course, depend on photosynthesis by plants to provide food from which we obtain carbon to "burn" with oxygen in our bodies; even when we eat meat, we are only eating plants at secondhand.) Without free oxygen in the atmosphere, respiration would not work, and human life—among others—would be impossible. And without oxygen in the atmosphere, there would be no ozone layer, intense ultraviolet light would penetrate to the ground, and there would be no prospect of life like us surviving on the surface of the Earth. According to some calculations, even a modest reduction in the concentration of the ozone layer could have severe effects, especially, but not exclusively, on light-skinned people, today.

CANCER, CROPS AND CATTLE

People outside scientific circles began to sit up and take notice of supposed threats to the ozone layer when these were linked with the emotive word *cancer* in the early 1970s. Life, including human life, is particularly sensitive to ultraviolet radiation in the wavelength band from about 290 nm to 320 nm—so much so that this radiation band is called *biologically active* ultraviolet, also known as UV-B. It is, as we have seen, just in the part of the spectrum where ozone in the stratosphere absorbs most, but not all, of the radiation passing through. UV-B is a small part of the solar radiation that reaches the ground. It is more intense high on the slopes of mountains, where there is less troposphere above to finish the job of absorbing the UV, and in the tropics, where the Sun shines down with full force. Radiation with wavelengths below 290 nm, which is completely absorbed by stratospheric ozone today, can destroy nucleic acids (RNA and DNA) and protein, the basic molecules of life; in the band from 240 nm to 290 nm it is called UV-C. Nobody can say for sure what would be the consequences of letting this radiation through to the ground. But because UV-B does reach the ground, and more strongly in some places than others, it is possible to get a good rule-of-thumb guide to what would happen if the intensity increased by a few percent, simply by comparing different regions of the globe today.

UV-B causes sunburn, and people who are exposed to more UV-B are more likely to develop certain forms of skin cancer, including one called *malignant melanoma*, which is often fatal. By comparing the cancer statistics from different regions, researchers working for the U.S. Environmental Protection Agency (EPA) have calculated that for every 1 percent decrease in the concentration of ozone in the stratosphere there would be a 5 percent increase in the number of nonmalignant skin cancers each year in the United States—an additional 10,000 to 20,000 victims over and above the present figures. These cancers are distressing, but can usually be removed surgically without ill effects. The more serious malignant melanomas are less closely linked with UV-B, but there are indications that each 1 percent increase in the radiation would increase mortality from the disease by about 1 percent. In the 1970s, the average annual incidence of malignant melanoma in the United States was about 4.2 cases for every 100,000 people. It represented a threat about as severe as breast cancer and was responsible for roughly 1 percent of all cancer deaths.

But none of these cancers develops immediately; they occur later in life as a result of exposure to UV-B over a period of time. Exposure to the radiation now stores up problems for both individuals and the medical profession in decades to come.

In fact, the incidence of malignant melanoma has been increasing in virtually all countries in recent decades. This is probably because of changing fashions, both in the sense that modern clothes expose larger areas of our bodies to the Sun than did the clothes of generations past, and because people today are more likely to spend time sunbathing—an idea that would have been incomprehensible to Victorian ladies, who cultivated a pale and interesting complexion as a sign that they did not have to toil for a living. Remember, too, that people are living longer these days, and as other diseases are conquered there is more chance for something like malignant melanoma to show up in old age. Toilers in the fields of the nineteenth century were likely to be dead of something else long before the age at which malignant melanoma shows up. Today, keeping out of the Sun may not be quite the answer to the problem, however, whether or not slightly more UV-B reaches the ground in the future. Some studies show that the cancers are more common among people who lead indoor lives but are intermittently exposed to intense UV-B for short periods of time, as when office workers fly south each year for their vacation. An all-year-round tan seems to provide at least some protection from the damaging radiation—which is little comfort if you are an office worker.

Skin cancer is, however, now seen as just one risk among many to human health posed by increased exposure to UV-B. The radiation also suppresses the activity of the human immune system, the body's natural defense mechanism. One effect of this would be to make it easier for tumors to grow without the body's fighting back effectively. Other effects, according to an EPA report published in 1987, include the likelihood of increased incidence of infections by herpes virus, hepatitis, and infections of the skin caused by parasites. These are all problems that affect people of all skin colors, unlike the skin cancer problem, which is worse for people with fair skin. Nobody has yet been able to put figures on how much any of these problems might increase for each percentage point increase in the amount of UV-B reaching the ground. In yet another study, however, Sidney Lerman of Emory University at Atlanta, Georgia, claims that a 1 percent decrease in the amount of ozone overhead would increase the number of victims of cataracts of the eye in the United States by 25,000. The message from all these studies is the same—human health suffers if the ozone layer is depleted.

What of other animals, and plants? Most plants simply have not been tested for the effects of increased UV-B, but of 200 that have, two-thirds showed at least some sensitivity. Soybeans, one of the key crops of modern agriculture, suffer a 25 percent decrease in yield when UV-B is increased by 25 percent. In the oceans, phytoplankton, the tiny floating organisms that are at the base of the food chain, also seem to suffer from increased exposure to UV-B, and the larval stages of some fish are known to be sensitive to the radiation. Species now fished commercially might suffer, putting additional strain on other sources of food for the world's growing population. Even that favorite of the ecological movement, the whale, would be at risk if the krill they feed on were adversely affected by increased UV-B.

As for domesticated food animals, research has already shown that cattle suffer from an increase in ailments known as *cancer eye* and *pink eye* when exposed to more UV-B; the effects on wild animals and uncultivated vegetation over the Earth can, as yet, only be guessed at.

Although the effects of a significant increase in UV-B are clearly negative, it might seem that there is little or no cause for concern if natural fluctuations can change the concentration of ozone considerably from month to month or year to year (or decade to decade), and if there is a wide range of exposure to UV-B already from the poles to equator. How big does a change have to be to be significant? Over Philadelphia, for example, the amount of UV-B arriving in summer is six times the amount arriving in winter. But complacency is misplaced. If the average concentration of ozone declined by one or two percent, which might not even be detectable against the "noise" of natural fluctuations, there would still be an increase in the average intensity of UV-B reaching each part of the globe over a long period of time. If you are not convinced that this matters, consider the equivalent kind of change in temperature. A change of 6 degrees F from day to day, or from day to night, is common—nothing to get excited about. But a shift of 6 degrees F in the global average temperature would, in one direction, plunge us back into a full ice age, or, in the other direction, melt the polar ice caps and inundate cities such as New York, London, and Leningrad.

The same kind of analogy helps to understand the regional significance of ozone depletion. The average annual temperature in Houston, for example, is just about 70 degrees F; in Chicago it is just about 50 degrees F. People live in both cities and get on pretty well. Some may choose to move from Houston to Chicago, where the temperature is 20 degrees lower. If they do, life continues. But it would be very different if the whole world were to cool by 20 degrees F.* And even if there are large natural fluctuations in the ozone concentration, a reduction in the average concentration would mean that at the times of greatest downward fluctuation in the continuing natural pattern of changes, more UV-B would reach the surface of the Earth than any organisms now living here have ever experienced.

So the ozone layer, a layer of poison around our globe, is very much linked with the presence of life on

---

*I have borrowed these temperature analogies from *The Ozone War*, which recounts the story of the ozone controversies of the early and middle 1970s (see bibliography, p. 183).

Earth. It is important to us personally; but it is also a sign of life, a planetary proclamation that Earth, out of all the planets in our Solar System, harbors living things. To us, fire is something we take for granted. But in the Universe at large, a planet that has an atmosphere so rich in a reactive chemical like oxygen that combustion can take place freely on its surface is an anomaly. The natural state of a chemical system left to its own devices is to see all possible reactions such as combustion take place, leaving the active ingredients locked up in stable compounds. Gases like carbon dioxide are indeed stable and do not react violently with most other substances. An intelligent alien being, visiting our Solar System, could study the atmospheres of Venus and Mars from afar, note that they are composed chiefly of carbon dioxide, and conclude that they were stable systems, with nothing much going on there. But the same observations of Earth from afar would show an atmosphere rich in oxygen, which ought to be locked up by chemical reactions, and traces of the even more reactive ozone. Such an atmosphere is chemically unstable, in a dynamic balance of some kind, not in stable equilibrium. It would be an obvious place to look for interesting biological processes at work.

And how much ozone is there in the crucial layer that shields us from uncomfortable, or lethal, exposure to solar ultraviolet? In the layer of the atmosphere from about 9 to 30 miles—more than twice the thickness, in terms of altitude, of the troposphere in which we live—there may be about four or five billion tons of ozone. If all that gas could be brought down to sea level and spread evenly around the globe, atmospheric pressure would squash it into a layer only about a tenth of an inch thick. It doesn't seem like a great deal of gas to do such an important job. However, the thickness of the whole atmosphere of the Earth, compared with the size of our planet, is no more than the thickness of the skin of an apple, compared with the size of the apple.

In the industrialized world, a journey of 10 miles is scarcely of any significance; some people commute to work across much greater distances each day, while others would regard a hike of 10 miles as a nice weekend opportunity to stretch their legs and admire the scenery. Going 10 miles straight up, however, requires great technological ingenuity (it is where the Concorde flies) and takes us to the heart of the stratosphere, which is itself on the fringes of space. People first realized that there might be a human threat to the ozone layer, with all that implies, when aerospace technology advanced to the point where flights to such awesome vertical distances began to look like a routine possibility.

CHAPTER TWO

A SUPERSONIC RED HERRING?

The Concorde—the Anglo-French supersonic transport aircraft (SST)—is often regarded as something of a flying white elephant. Built in small numbers, and flown only by the national carriers of the two countries that developed it, the aircraft can be described as profitable only by taking a biased view of its day-to-day operating costs, and writing off its enormous development costs and pretending they had never been paid. In the story of the developing understanding of the potential for human activities to damage the ozone layer, however, the Concorde appears more as a supersonic red herring. The fact that the aircraft was being developed, and the possibility of the development of a rival American SST, prompted calculations that suggested that enough aircraft of this kind, flying at altitudes of about 9 miles and above, might do irreparable damage to the ozone layer. Later calculations showed that the harmful effects would not be as great as originally feared, and with so few SSTs ever having become operational, that specific problem went away of its own accord.

But the issues raised spilled over into a broader debate about the impact of human activities on the ozone layer—and there is always a risk that some future government might be tempted to sanction the development of fleets of super SSTs. There are, indeed, some signs of this already, with discussions both in the United States and Europe today about hypersonic vehicles that could take off like ordinary aircraft but could fly into orbit around the Earth like the space shuttle; and the shuttle itself, if it ever flies often enough, could also destroy significant quantities of ozone on its way through the stratosphere. So there is no cause for complacency, and every reason to spell out the details of the first ozone debate, as a warning for the future.

FLYING INTO TROUBLE

The ozone debate began with the work of James Mc-Donald, of the University of Arizona. During the 1960s, he carried out an investigation of some of the likely environmental impacts of SSTs, at the request of the U.S. National Academy of Sciences (NAS). At that time, people concerned at the prospect of fleets of aircraft flying through the stratosphere had pointed out the possibility that the water vapor released by the aircraft (one of the exhaust products from its engines) might produce large condensation trails and clouds of fine ice crystals that would be slow to disperse and might alter the climate of the Earth, by reflecting away heat from the Sun before it could penetrate to the troposphere. McDonald was a member of the Academy's panel on weather and climate modification, and he was an expert on ice crystals in the atmosphere. He carried out calculations that showed that this feared climatic impact of a fleet of SSTs would not in fact be a serious problem, and the conclusions were published in 1966.

By the end of the 1960s, work on the Concorde (and its Russian "copycat" equivalent, the Tupolev 144) was going ahead, and Boeing was proceeding with its plans for a superior American SST, which would fly higher and faster than the Concorde and carry more passengers; it was dubbed the 2707. The Academy asked McDonald to take another look at the way such SSTs might affect the stratosphere, and it was during this work that he realized that the aircraft might have the potential to destroy ozone.

The way in which an aircraft might destroy ozone is easy to see in broad principle but hard to calculate in precise detail. Any engine that breathes in large quantities of air and uses the oxygen in it to burn fuel at a high temperature inevitably produces oxides of nitrogen among its exhaust gases—after all, nitrogen is by far the most common constituent of the atmosphere. Oxides of nitrogen are collectively dubbed NO_x by the atmospheric chemists and come in various forms; the simplest, nitric oxide (NO), is, as we have seen, an efficient scavenger of ozone, and other nitrogen oxides also play a part in reactions that remove ozone from the stratosphere. From the fuel itself, the engines also produce oxides of hydrogen, which include water, and which the chemists collectively dub HO_x. Water itself does not destroy ozone, but the hydroxyl radical, HO, does, through a similar set of reactions to the ones involving NO. McDonald himself wasn't concerned about the effects of NO_x on the stratosphere, but he began to be worried that HO_x might have a serious effect on the ozone layer.

In 1970, there seemed a serious possibility that SSTs would become established as a major means of transport, operating especially on the prime North Atlantic routes. People in the aircraft industry talked of a fleet of eight hundred Boeing SSTs operating between 1985 and 1990; when McDonald used that figure in his calculations, he concluded that the operation of this fleet would cause a reduction of 4 percent in the concentration of ozone in the stratosphere. In presenting this conclusion, he pointed out that a 1 percent decrease in ozone concentrations would cause an additional 5,000 to 10,000 cases of skin cancer annually in the United States alone—not 5,000 or 10,000 new cases altogether, but that many new cases *each year*. Highly concerned by his discovery of a link between SST operations and cancer, McDonald reported his conclusions to both the Academy and the Department of Transportation before the end of 1970. In March 1971 he expressed his concerns publicly, as an expert witness at congressional hearings on a bill to continue funding for the Boeing SST project. His presentation was emotional and sometimes difficult to follow, and observers reported that he seemed out to "make a case" against the SST, rather than simply to present the scientific facts and let them speak for themselves. McDonald won no friends at the hearings, but the problem was now out in the open, and soon became the subject of broader scientific debate.

Other researchers before McDonald had, in fact, published calculations of the effects of both HO_x and NO_x on the stratosphere, but these had not gained widespread notice. The oxides of both hydrogen and nitrogen occur naturally in the environment and were of interest to scientists studying the stratosphere even before the SST came on the scene. John Hampson, an Englishman working in Canada, had tackled the HO_x problem, and so had a Boeing researcher, Halstead Harrison, who published figures similar to McDonald's in November 1970 but drew no alarming conclusions from them. Also in 1970, Paul Crutzen, a Dutch-born scientist who has worked in several countries, pointed out the importance of catalytic chains involving NO_x—he even made the link with SSTs, pointing out that the projected fleet of these aircraft would inject as much NO_x into the stratosphere as natural processes do. But he was then still a junior researcher, originally trained in meteorology, not chemistry, who hesitated to push his ideas forward in the scientific marketplace. He didn't have the opportunity to testify before a congressional hearing, and, crucially, he didn't take the step that McDonald made, linking ozone depletion with cancer.

By the time McDonald made his splash, a panel set up by the Department of Commerce Technical Advisory Board was investigating the scientific evidence for the likely impact of the proposed SST fleet on the environment. Stratospheric chemistry was not, initially, one of the main concerns of the panel, but it included a chemist, Joe Hirschfelder, of the University of Wisconsin, who pushed the other members into convening a scientific meeting on the topic. It was held in Boulder, Colorado, on March 18 and 19, 1971, and it was there that the potential importance of NO_x from SST exhausts first gained wide recognition.

The breakthrough came from Harold Johnston, of the University of California at Berkeley, who had been investigating the problem of photochemical smog near the ground, where NO_x actually helps in the production of ozone. McDonald had presented his calculations involving HO_x on the first day of the meeting and been roundly abused by his audience for dragging cancer into the discussion. Although now his work is respected and acknowledged, McDonald received a rough time all through the early part of 1971, from congressmen, the press, and his scientific colleagues. His ozone work was tarred with the brush of his interest in UFOs, which caused widespread derision, even though all he said was that UFO claims should be investigated scientifically, to settle the issue one way or the other. He committed suicide that summer, although there is no proof that this was a result of his involvement in the battles about ozone.

On the second day of the meeting, Johnston presented a detailed analysis of the NO_x chemistry of the stratosphere—he was not aware of Crutzen's work of the year before—and concluded that although there were many uncertainties, operating a fleet of five hundred SSTs for two years would reduce the ozone concentration of the stratosphere by at least 10 percent, and maybe by much more. In debate following the formal presentations, his colleagues agreed, somewhat reluctantly, that he had identified a potentially serious, and neglected, aspect of the way SST emissions would affect stratospheric chemistry. Largely as a result of this meeting in Boulder, the panel reported back to the secretary of commerce that the SST could not be given a clean bill of environmental health, and that more research would be needed on the chemistry of the stratosphere before it would be possible to decide "whether or not a large number of flights of supersonic transports would cause significant environmental hazard to mankind."[*]

The SST project was already in financial trouble, and about to be killed off by Congress. Boeing never got the money it requested, which would have enabled it to build two prototypes of the new aircraft. The "scare" linking SSTs, ozone, and skin cancer was not a decisive factor; rather, this decision was made largely on economic grounds. But the cancer scare made headlines, it introduced the idea of the fragility of the ozone layer to a wide public, and it started at least some scientists working more intensely than ever before on the study of stratospheric chemistry, trying to determine which chemical reactions were important (and how fast they occur in the stratosphere), and which ones could be neglected. This is a tricky process, in-

---

Quoted by Dotto and Schiff, p. 57 (see bibliography, p. 183).

volving many hours of calculation on modern computers, and skillful measurements of the rates at which chemicals react under different conditions in the laboratory. With better computers, and better chemistry, the numbers that came out of the calculations were bound to change as the years passed, but hopefully they would be steadily improved.

The ball really started rolling in August 1971, when Johnston's calculations, essentially as presented to the Boulder meeting, were published in the journal *Science*, pointing out to the scientific community at large that the real problem raised by SSTs flying through the stratosphere was the release of NO_x, not HO_x. The definitive statement on the issue, in the light of available chemical knowledge, came in 1974, following a three-year research program that involved a thousand scientists from ten countries and cost $21 million. Organized by the U.S. Department of Transportation and called the Climatic Impact Assessment Program (CIAP), it concluded that a fleet of five hundred Boeing 2707s cruising for seven or eight hours per day in the stratosphere, each emitting about half an ounce of nitric oxide for every 2 and a quarter pounds of fuel burned, would cause an overall reduction in the ozone concentration of the stratosphere of the Northern Hemisphere of about 15 percent. Even the Southern Hemisphere would suffer a depletion of about 8 percent, although few SSTs would be flying there. Johnston was right, and in a way McDonald was vindicated (although he had been wrong about the importance of HO_x) by the implication in the CIAP report that each Boeing 2707 that became operational would have caused an increased incidence of several hundred skin cancers each year, and ultimately several deaths. But the question was largely academic by the middle of the 1970s, with no prospect of such fleets of SSTs becoming operational in the immediate future, and plenty of other reasons for concern about the ozone layer. Although the arguments were raised time and again in the battle over whether the Concorde should be granted landing rights in North America, by the end of the 1970s the SST issue was far from the forefront of public concern about the environment.

Had the public still been concerned about the effects of SSTs on ozone, they might have been surprised, and more than a little puzzled, when improved calculations (better chemistry and better computer models) suggested in 1977 that existing designs of these aircraft might, after all, have little effect on the stratosphere. The change happened because the new calculations shifted the expected height in the atmosphere at which NO_x reactions stop favoring the production of ozone, as they do in smog zones, and switch over to destroying ozone, which they do high in the stratosphere, where conditions are very different (and where there is ozone to be destroyed). The Concorde flies barely in the bottom fringes of the stratosphere, at around 9 miles. The earlier calculations had implied a switchover of the NO_x effects from favoring ozone to destroying ozone at about 6 miles, so that the Concorde's emissions would have been well in the destruction zone. The later figures put the changeover at the bottom of the stratosphere itself, so that at Concorde altitudes NO_x is now seen as only a minor threat to ozone. By the time this was discovered, however, another vehicle that flies even higher was coming off the drawing board. The space shuttle, by its very nature, flies right through the stratosphere, and it belches out a huge amount of exhaust. What effect might *that* have on ozone?

SHUTTLING CHLORINE
INTO THE STRATOSPHERE

The SST initiated widespread scientific debate about the impact of human activities on the ozone layer. The space shuttle introduced a new element into the debate—chlorine. Chlorine (although not chlorine from the space shuttle) is now implicated in the opening up of the hole in the sky over Antarctica, a hole bigger than the continental United States. But the way chlorine was shuffled into the debate, almost through the back door, represents one of the most bizarre twists to the whole ozone story.

If the original proposal for a fully reusable space shuttle had gone ahead, the chlorine problem would not have surfaced in this connection at all. At the start of the 1970s, NASA favored the development of a two-stage system in which an orbiter, the size of a medium-range airliner, would ride piggyback on a booster the size of a 747. Both vehicles would be piloted, and both would be able to fly back to land like conventional aircraft. The booster would have been powered by twelve rocket engines, burning liquid hydrogen and liquid oxygen to lift the paired vehicles from the ground. When these had exhausted their fuel, the orbiter would break away and continue into space, using its own hydrogen/oxygen-fueled rockets, leaving the booster to fly back to base under the power of its auxiliary jet engines.

Such a plan was ambitious and expensive. It fell by the wayside, and NASA had to fall back on a cheaper compromise, the partly reusable shuttle system that came into operation at the end of the 1970s. This is basically equivalent to the orbiter stage of the original proposal, using its own rocket motors and the fuel from a huge external tank to get into orbit. In order to lift the required weight of liquid oxygen and liquid hydrogen off the ground and give the vehicle enough boost to reach orbit, however, it required a pair of additional solid-fuel rockets strapped on to the shuttle/tank configuration for launch. The now-familiar TV image of a shuttle blasting off from the Cape and soaring high into the sky, where the two expended solid-fuel rockets fall away, is the result of compromises forced by economics. The same compromises are responsible for the presence of the external fuel tank, which is also jettisoned by the shuttle before it reaches orbit. It was a combination of faults in the solid-fuel boosters and the proximity of this huge tank of hydrogen and oxygen—a bomb waiting to be ignited—that led to the *Challenger* disaster and the grounding of the shuttle. All that lay far in the future, however, when several teams working in the United States independently began to worry about one of the waste products that would be released from the solid-fuel boosters as the shuttle climbed through the stratosphere.

One of the gases released by the burning of the solid-fuel rockets is hydrogen chloride (HC1). These rockets burn until the vehicle is well into the stratosphere, and the empty rocket casings are only released from the shuttle/tank configuration at an altitude of about 31 miles. The decision to use the solid-fuel boosters was made early in 1972, and by the summer of that year NASA had produced an environmental-impact statement that specifically mentioned that HC1 would be spread along the shuttle's path from ground level into the high stratosphere, and that most of the hydrogen chloride released would be deposited in the stratosphere. One shuttle flight a week (the NASA planners were optimistic in the early 1970s) would deposit more than 5,000 tons of HC1 in the stratosphere each year. However, although the document looked in some detail at the effects of HC1 in the troposphere (concluding that there was no significant environmental risk), it failed to make the connection between HC1 and ozone.

This is not really so surprising, since the statement was drafted even before discussions got going on the impact of SSTs on the stratosphere, and in 1972 nobody was worrying about the effects of chlorine and chlorine compounds on the ozone layer. Space scientists didn't realize that chlorine atoms are efficient ozone scavengers; chemists didn't know that the shuttle boosters would emit HCl. Even so, the environmental-impact statement was recognized as an incomplete first cut at the problem, and NASA realized that more research on the way shuttle flights might affect the atmosphere was needed. A team of scientists at the University of Michigan got the job of trying to determine what aspects of environmental impact the original statement may have overlooked.

That team included Richard Stolarski and Ralph Cicerone, two young researchers who had no background in chemistry (Stolarski had trained in physics, Cicerone in electrical engineering), but who saw the developing excitement in stratospheric studies and wanted a piece of the action. They are now senior researchers who have been involved in all aspects of the continuing debate about the ozone layer since 1973, and they are now making major contributions to the study of the hole over Antarctica. Their careers have built from that NASA contract to look into the effects of the shuttle on the environment—but initially it was far from being plain sailing. Dotto and Schiff tell how the two neophytes gradually learned enough chemistry to begin to appreciate that chlorine in the stratosphere might pose a problem for ozone—and how, unknown to them, parallel studies were being carried out at the Palo Alto Research Laboratory, where a team had been assigned the task, under the CIAP study, of investigating engine exhausts in general. The Palo Alto team included rocket engines in their research, and was alerted to the importance of chlorine by Harold Johnston.

When the Michigan team alerted NASA to the

possibility that shuttle exhausts might damage the ozone layer, they came under heavy pressure to keep quiet about their work, at least until more could be discovered about the chains of reactions involving chlorine. This had the strange result that at a meeting in Kyoto, Japan, in 1973, where experts debated the chemistry of the stratosphere, Stolarski presented a summary of the work on chlorine in the stratosphere, which failed to mention the shuttle at all, but suggested that volcanic eruptions might provide the chlorine. In spite of this, when Cicerone and Stolarski prepared a full description of their work for publication in *Science*, and included specific mention of the shuttle problem, they once again came under pressure from NASA and were urged to withdraw the paper from publication. The paper was, in fact, rejected by the journal—expert reviewers, who vet all scientific papers before they appear in print, advised the editors that the work did not say anything new enough or interesting enough about stratospheric chemistry to merit publication. The review system is a good one most of the time, but, as you see, it is not infallible.

But all was not lost. The proceedings of the Kyoto meeting were about to be published by the *Canadian Journal of Chemistry*, and there was still (just) time for the Michigan team to get their full paper published there, not just the highlights Stolarski had presented in Japan. Curiously, it appeared almost alongside another paper drawing attention to the effects on the stratosphere of chlorine compounds from the shuttle exhausts. This paper had been written by Mike McElroy and Steve Wofsy, of Harvard University. McElroy had indeed been one of the main speakers at Kyoto, but he had talked there chiefly about the role of nitrogen oxides in the stratosphere, mentioning chlorine only in passing and the shuttle not at all, although he had in fact been working with Wofsy on the shuttle exhaust problem. He had even had a heated argument with

Stolarski in Kyoto about the claims that chlorine from volcanoes might affect the stratosphere. Harvard researchers, McElroy had told the meeting, had established that volcanic chlorine was not a problem. Both Stolarski and McElroy may have suspected, when they were wrangling about volcanoes, that the real problem was the shuttle—but neither had mentioned it. Both ended up publishing the shuttle work, not actually presented in Kyoto, in the official record of the proceedings of that conference. And for years afterward, the two teams, from Harvard and Michigan, had a deep distrust of each other as a result.

With the chlorine question out in the open, at least in the arena of scientific debate, if not in the awareness of the general public, NASA had to take steps, like it or not, to assess the implications. Although the research effort involved never reached the scale of the Climatic Impact Assessment Program study, by 1977 the evidence gathered by NASA, and independently by the National Academy of Sciences (NAS), suggested that the effect of sixty shuttle launches a year would be to reduce the concentration of ozone in the stratosphere over the Northern Hemisphere by only about 0.2 percent. Because of uncertainties in the calculations (for example, a lack of precise knowledge of the rates at which some reactions take place under stratospheric conditions), the effect might be three times bigger (0.6 percent) or three times smaller (0.07 percent) than this "best estimate." And because chlorine is released directly into the stratosphere by the shuttle, then locked up fairly quickly by chemical reactions into stable compounds that sink down into the troposphere, the studies showed that it would take only a few years for the ozone layer to recover if the shuttle stopped flying, or if the booster rockets were changed to a design that did not emit chemically active chlorine compounds.

Another red herring? Today, the numbers seem almost entirely academic. The prospect of sixty shuttle flights a year is remote, to say the least, and the effects involved—less than a 1 percent change in ozone concentrations—seem insignificant compared with the alarming discoveries over Antarctica, where half the ozone now disappears each spring. But there are lessons to be learned from the shuttle story. The space station is still on the political agenda, and if that project does go ahead it will require very many shuttle flights. The Soviet Union is developing its own space shuttle, and the European Space Agency has plans for a shuttle, and aspirations toward developing that hypersonic ramjet that takes off from a runway, breathes air on its way up through the troposphere and into the stratosphere, then switches over to rocket propulsion. Of course, none of these designs utilizes the solid-fuel rocket boosters that are responsible for the release of HCl on U.S. shuttle flights—but they would inject more NO_x, and more HO_x, into the stratosphere. The effects of any vehicle designed to fly above the tropopause should be examined very carefully before flights are allowed to begin, in light of what happened with the SSTs and the space shuttle. The more projects there are, the worse the situation becomes. A reduction of 1 percent in the ozone concentration might seem an acceptable risk for a single project, like the shuttle. But if ten projects each result in a 1 percent reduction, the overall concentration has decreased by 10 percent, without any single project being obviously to blame, or necessarily willing to accept the responsibility.

The shuttle brought chlorine into the debate, and it also brought NASA into the serious study of the stratosphere. The space agency was well equipped to study the ozone layer, both with satellites looking down from above and with ground-based and airborne instruments, and it was developing a pool of expertise in stratospheric chemistry as well. Maybe some other agency could have taken the lead in studying the ozone problem in the 1970s just as well; but by the time the hole over Antarctica was discovered, NASA was without doubt the best-equipped organization in the world to head the investigation. Nobody anticipated the need for that application of NASA's expertise, however, during the mid-1970s, when the public, which had been so concerned about the links between SSTs and skin cancer, took scarcely any notice of the discussions about the effects of the shuttle on the ozone layer. This was not due solely to NASA's other great skill—the agency's expertise in public relations and its success at playing down the problem. By the middle of 1974, the public had something much closer to home to worry about, and by 1975 the spray-can "war" was in full swing.

CHAPTER THREE

THE SPRAY-CAN WAR

Until the discovery of the hole over Antarctica, the most visible feature of the debate about the ozone layer had been the "war" between environmentalists and the manufacturers of aerosol sprays in the United States in the middle of the 1970s. It was a propaganda war, fought with words and chemical equations, but emotions sometimes seemed to run as high as in a real shooting war. The manufacturers had major investments and markets to protect; the environmentalists felt that the well-being of the whole planet was at stake. Somewhere in the middle were the scientists trying to assess the real extent of the problem, but tending, in many cases, to lean on the side of the environmentalists. After all, aerosol sprays are, in most cases, a luxury. It would do us no real harm to do without them, even if the threat to the ozone layer proved not to be that large.

An aerosol spray gets its name because it squirts out its contents as a fine mist of tiny droplets, called an aerosol. To a scientist, the particles form the aerosol, and aerosol particles occur naturally throughout the atmosphere, including the stratosphere, in many different forms. To a lay person, the term *aerosol* is synonymous with *spray can*, not with the fine mist of particles that emerges from the nozzle of the spray can. In addition, most nonscientists have no idea that the word *aerosol* might also be used to describe a hazy cloud of, say, nitric acid droplets floating many miles above the ground. So it may be best to avoid the term entirely here and stick to the more prosaic *spray can*.

Spray cans were *very* big business in the United States in 1974. The year before, 2.9 billion cans, half the world total, had been filled in North America with products ranging from hair spray and underarm deodorant to insecticides, paints, polishes, and disinfectants. About half of these spray cans used compounds known as chlorofluorocarbons, or CFCs, to push the active ingredients out of the can; when you pressed the nozzle, the CFC propellant rushed out through the tiny hole, carrying a fine mist of the active ingredient along with it.

For decades, CFCs had been regarded by the chemical industry as something of a miracle substance. Their unusual properties had been discovered more or less by accident at the end of the 1920s, when they were originally developed as the working fluid used in refrigerators. They seemed ideally suited to the task, since they boiled at between –40 degrees F and 32 degrees F, were nonflammable, nontoxic, cheap to manufacture, easy to store, and chemically stable. It is indeed precisely because they are very stable compounds that CFCs do not react either with oxygen, to burn, or with living things, to poison them. They seemed perfect for use as propellants in spray cans, and the first product of this kind using CFCs went on the market in 1950. They have also proved useful as solvents, effective at cleaning delicate semiconductor circuitry without attacking the plastic boards on which the circuits and chips are mounted, and in blowing foams of all kinds, from fire extinguisher foam to the foam insulation used in the walls of some houses, and the foamed hard plastic of disposable coffee cups and clamshell hamburger cartons. More of all that later. In 1974, and the following couple of years, it was CFCs' use in spray cans that hit the headlines.

LOVELOCK'S MISTAKE

CFCs had seemed too good to be true, and so it proved. A great deal of these chemicals were getting out into the environment and beginning to build up there. Seventy-five percent of the emissions to the air came from spray cans, which by their very nature had to release the propellant gases; about 15 percent came from leaky refrigeration and air-conditioning systems, especially car air conditioners. CFCs are so stable that they remain in the atmosphere for a very long time. There is nothing in the troposphere that can attack them and break down their chemical structure. They are so stable, indeed, that Jim Lovelock, the first scientist to investigate their distribution around the world, did so because he was interested in tracing the movement of air currents, and decided that CFCs would provide an excellent marker showing how air masses moved. At least, that was the "official" motive he gave in his scientific publications; in fact, Lovelock simply delighted in the opportunity to match his scientific wits against nature by designing and building instruments sensitive enough to sniff a trace of CFCs in the air from the surface of a ship in the middle of the ocean.

Lovelock resembles the image of a "natural philosopher" of bygone centuries more than he does a scientist of the late twentieth century. He is both independently minded and, literally, an independent researcher, who operates from his own laboratory at his home on the fringes of Dartmoor, in the southwest of England. But his expertise as an instrument designer and his reputation in the scientific community are sufficiently high for him to be paid a retainer by instrument manufacturers Hewlett-Packard, and to have contributed experiments to the *Viking* missions that landed probes on the surface of Mars—and he has also been elected a Fellow of the Royal Society. Today, he is best known as the father of the concept of Gaia, which envisages all the living systems of the Earth as part of one organism, Gaia, which has maintained a stable environment, suitable for life, for millions of years through the operation of natural feedback processes. Lovelock likens these feedbacks to the way the human body keeps itself at a constant temperature, even though the air temperature may vary widely.

The development of the concept of Gaia is very relevant to the current debate about the damage mankind may be doing to the atmospheric environment and the likely consequences for life on Earth. In the early 1970s, however, it was CFCs that had Lovelock's attention. After building and testing a CFC sniffer at his home (then in Wiltshire), he scrounged a lift on the research vessel *Shackleton*, and during 1971 and 1972 made a voyage from Britain to Antarctica and back, checking out the concentration of CFCs in the air all the way there and all the way back. This was no mean achievement, and colleagues speak admiringly of the "exquisite sensitivity" of Lovelock's instrument, which measured the abundances in units of parts per 10^{12} (that is, parts per trillion). In the early 1970s, the concentrations of CFCs in the atmosphere ranged from a few to a few dozen in these units, and Lovelock could not only detect them, he could tell you how the concentration of each of the two main CFCs varied from the North Atlantic to the South Pacific. He published the results of his measurements in the journal *Nature* early in 1973, and in so doing made a blunder that still causes him to shake his head ruefully when it is drawn to his attention (as it was at the recent Dahlem meeting). After pointing out the potential usefulness of CFCs as a means to trace the movement of air masses, Lovelock commented in that paper "the presence of these compounds constitutes no conceivable hazard."

Lovelock has never been what he calls "a doomwatch sort of person," and he was anxious not to stir unnecessary alarm. Inert, nonpoisonous CFCs certainly do not pose any conceivable threat in the troposphere at the concentrations Lovelock had measured, and that is what, he now acknowledges, he should have said in the *Nature* paper. Increasing amounts of CFCs, building up inexorably and then being transported up into the stratosphere, would pose a very real threat indeed.* But nobody, including Lovelock, appreciated this immediately in 1973. Lovelock's meticulous measurements and his dogmatic statement (almost a red rag to some bullish scientists) both served, however, to set wheels turning.

The potential problem with CFCs is that they contain chlorine. Indeed, the full name for this class of compounds, chlorofluorocarbons, indicates that they are built up from atoms of chlorine, fluorine, and carbon. Du Pont, the major manufacturer of CFCs, gave their own products the brand name Freons, and developed a labeling system that indicates, to the cognoscenti, how many atoms of each kind are present in a particular

---

*They also pose a conceivable, all too easily conceivable, hazard by their presence in the troposphere, through their contribution to the greenhouse effect, which is discussed later.

type of Freon. This system* is now widely used for all CFCs; a shorthand naming system has evolved in which the two most commonly used CFCs are known as F-11 and F-12—their full chemical names are trichlorofluoromethane (CCl_3F) and dichlorofluoromethane (CCl_2F_2). Others that are important to the debate today are F-22 ($CHClF_2$) and F-113 ($C_2Cl_3F_3$). F-11, it is now estimated, survives for 75 years before being broken down in the atmosphere, and F-12 for 110 years—so pollution being caused by release of these products now, in the late 1980s, will still be affecting our planet at the end of the twenty-first century, even if CFC emissions are halted tomorrow.

It was this kind of realization, plus the bald statement by Lovelock that CFCs posed "no conceivable hazard," that set some scientists thinking. One was Charles Kolb, a chemist based in Boston, who realized that the compounds must eventually release chlorine, but did not know, at first, that chlorine could scavenge ozone. It was only in September 1973, when he heard from Mike McElroy about the discussions of chlorine in the stratosphere at the Kyoto meeting, that something began to click. Before Kolb could set seriously to work on the problem, however, the main scientific protaganist in the spray-can war had begun to make a noise.

ROWLAND RAISES THE PROBLEM

In 1972, Sherry Rowland was a scientist who had already made his name as a chemist who specialized in

---

*The first digit in the number indicates how many fluorine atoms (F) are in each molecule; the second is the number of hydrogen atoms (H), *plus 1;* the third is the number of carbon atoms (C), *minus 1,* and is omitted if it is equal to zero. All the other atoms required by the chemical rules must then be chlorine (Cl), so no chemist needs that number to be spelled out.

the study of radioactive isotopes. He was based at the University of California at Irvine, but traveled widely to scientific conferences and meetings related to his work—and sometimes to those that were not really relevant to his main line of research but looked as if they might prove interesting. It was out of general scientific curiosity that he attended a meeting held in Florida in January 1972, which, although organized by the U.S. Atomic Energy Commission, was concerned with atmospheric chemistry, which was not Rowland's main interest at the time. The formal presentations at that meeting made no great impression on the visitor from California, but an item of gossip he picked up during one of the breaks from the formal presentations roused his curiosity and stuck in his mind.

A little earlier, in 1971, Lester Machta, who worked with the U.S. National Oceanic and Atmospheric Administration (NOAA), had been at another conference where atmospheric chemistry was discussed, and both Jim Lovelock and Ray McCarthy, of Du Pont, were also present. The three of them got into conversation about Lovelock's early work with the CFC sniffer (before he made his voyage to Antarctica and back, and long before any details of that global study were published), and Lovelock asked McCarthy, who ran Du Pont's Freon lab, how much of the various forms of Freon had been produced and released into the atmosphere since they had come into production. McCarthy's rough estimate turned out to be very close to the total burden of CFCs in the atmosphere indicated by Lovelock's measurements. None of the three scientists regarded this as anything more than an interesting tidbit of information. But when Machta mentioned it to Rowland at the Florida meeting in January 1972, the news tickled something at the back of his mind. If Lovelock's measurements showed that all the CFCs ever released were still in the troposphere, that meant nothing was destroying them in the lowest layer of the atmosphere. But they had to go somewhere, and the only place they could go was upward, into the stratosphere. Strong ultraviolet radiation will break up any molecule, and if the CFCs went high enough into the stratosphere they would have to decompose. Rowland remembers saying to Machta at the time, "Of course, it will always decompose with ultraviolet."* But this was only a casual thought and a passing comment; Rowland had no idea at the time that CFCs might pose a hazard to the environment, and it was eighteen months before the casual thought began to grow into something more elaborate.

By the summer of 1973, Lovelock's detailed results from his long voyage had been published in *Nature*, and Rowland was making his research plans for the following academic year. He obtained permission from the Atomic Energy Commission, which had been funding his research since 1956, to branch out into a study of CFCs, with the aim at the time of laying some ground rules so that if and when atmospheric scientists took up Lovelock's proposal to use the gases to trace the movement of air masses around the globe, they would know at least something about the way these compounds behaved in the atmospheric environment. Rowland knew about the ozone debate, then focusing on the SST issue, and had discussed it with Harold Johnston. But he did not immediately make a connection between CFCs percolating up into the stratosphere and being broken down by ultraviolet radiation, thereby becoming a threat to the ozone layer.

In the fall of 1973, a young researcher who had just completed his Ph.D. at the Berkeley campus of the University of California came to work with Rowland at Irvine. Mario Molina (who was born in Mexico) knew nothing about atmospheric chemistry—his research to date had been on chemical lasers. But once the CFC

---

*Quoted by Dotto and Schiff, p. 12 (see bibliography, p. 183).

story had been presented to him, with Lovelock's figures showing that all the CFCs ever released were still floating about in the troposphere, he shared Rowland's curiosity about the ultimate fate of these unusual chemicals. The two of them set out, with Rowland pointing the way and Molina, as is the fate of all fresh postdoctoral researchers, doing the donkey work, to determine once and for all what really would happen to the CFCs in the atmosphere.

It hardly took any time at all for Molina to establish that, indeed, *nothing* happened to them in the troposphere. CFCs do not interact with living things, they do not dissolve in the oceans, they do not get washed out of the air by rain—they do nothing at all except float around and gradually work their way upward, ultimately into the stratosphere. Within a few weeks of starting their new project, by November 1973 (when Charles Kolb was starting to think along the same lines

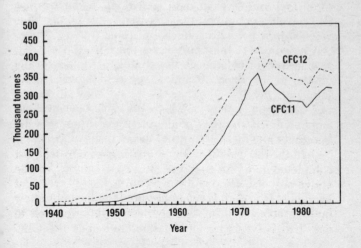

over in Boston), Rowland and Molina knew that CFCs would reach the stratosphere. It was a simple matter of textbook chemistry to deduce that they would be broken apart by ultraviolet radiation, releasing chlorine atoms. A few chlorine atoms in the stratosphere hardly seemed something to worry about—until Molina sat down and worked out the catalytic chains (already known, of course, to other scientists) by which a single chlorine atom can scavenge and destroy many thousands of ozone molecules.

The Kyoto meeting had been held in September 1973, and while Rowland and Molina were working through the problem to arrive independently at the conclusion that chlorine released by the breakdown of CFCs might damage the ozone layer, both the Michigan and the Harvard teams were working on their scientific papers that would "break" the story of chlorine from the space shuttle as a threat to stratospheric ozone. But Rowland and Molina knew nothing of this when they ran through the calculations, assuming that CFCs would continue to be released at a rate of about 800,000 tons per year (the rate of release in 1972) and concluded that within thirty years there would be half a million tons of chlorine in the stratosphere as a result, destroying between 20 and 40 percent of the ozone shield.

The basic chemistry, which has since been studied in great detail and is in no doubt at all (although some of the numbers for the *rates* of the reactions have been improved, the reactions themselves are known to occur), is indeed very simple. F-11, F-12, and F-113 do not absorb radiation with wavelengths longer than 240 nm, and so they are protected from photodecomposition in the troposphere by the presence of the ozone layer above. But once the CFCs percolate up to altitudes above 12.5 miles, they are exposed to ultraviolet radiation with wavelengths in the range of 200 to 220 nm. Taking the two most common CFCs (F-11, CCl_3F; F-12,

CCl_2F_2) as examples, we can see what happens when they decompose:

$$CCl_3F + UV \rightarrow Cl + CCl_2F$$
$$CCl_2F_2 + UV \rightarrow Cl + CClF_2$$

The presence of the free chlorine poses an obvious hazard to ozone in the stratosphere, once the existence of the chlorine catalytic chain is recognized:

$$Cl + O_3 \rightarrow ClO + O_2$$
$$ClO + O \rightarrow Cl + O_2$$

with the net effect

$$O + O_3 \rightarrow O_2 + O_2$$

but this is not the only threat, because the remaining fragments of CFCs, the CCl_2F and the $CClF_2$, are also chemically active and will react quickly with other atmospheric molecules. The basic chemical reason for this activity is that the fragments contain, overall, an odd number of electrons. It is a fundamental rule of nature that electrons "like" to pair up with each other, so that molecules or atoms that contain an even number of electrons are more stable—less reactive—than those that contain an odd number of electrons. All of the most abundant gases in the air, including nitrogen (N_2), oxygen (O_2), argon (Ar), carbon dioxide (CO_2), and water (H_2O), are even-electron species. So, indeed, are the very stable CFCs. Chlorine atoms (Cl), however, have an odd number of electrons, which is one reason why they tend to pair up with each other to form chlorine molecules (Cl_2). But where they cannot find other chlorine atoms to latch on to, individual chlorine atoms will try to pull an electron away from any obliging molecule that they bump into. Since the atom that the electron "belongs" to is bound to it by electric forces, it has to come along as well when the chlorine atom grabs hold of the electron. This is what makes the oxygen atom stick to the chlorine atom in ClO—but when there are other free oxygen atoms around for the oxygen atom in the ClO to pair up with, it does so because the attraction between two oxygen atoms is even greater than the attraction between a chlorine atom and an oxygen atom. The Cl is therefore released to search once again for a partner, and to break up another ozone molecule.

By knocking an odd-electron chlorine atom out of a chlorofluorocarbon, ultraviolet radiation leaves behind an odd-electron fragment, which will also react if possible in an attempt to restore a balanced pairing of electrons. The fragments, known as free radicals, go through a series of reactions involving oxygen, and ultimately release more chlorine atoms into the stratosphere, exacerbating the ozone problem.

When Rowland and Molina first calculated how big the problem would be, they didn't believe their figures. Persuaded that they had made a mistake, Rowland called Harold Johnston to get a second opinion, and learned from him about the work on the stratospheric chlorine chain that had been prompted by the shuttle studies. Convinced that they were indeed not making some stupid mistake in their chemistry or their calculations, the Irvine team wrote up a report of their work and sent it to *Nature*, where it was published in June 1974. A commentary drawing attention to the importance of the paper appeared in the same issue of *Nature*, and spelled out that "if the conclusions of Molina and Rowland are correct, then the effects of the stratospheric photodissociation of CF_2Cl_2 and $CFCl_3$ could not be removed immediately even if no more Freons were introduced at ground level. That is because of the postulated long residence time of these species in the lower atmosphere."* But in Britain at least, this was seen as interesting news for scientists, not for the general public, and any hazards were perceived as remote problems for the future. At the time, I was on the staff

---

*Nature 249 (June 28, 1974) p. 797: The overall tone of the commentary—second on the editoral pages, following a discussion of work on carcinogenic substances such as asbestos and PVC—was so cautious as to be almost apologetic.

of *Nature*, responsible for the Nature-Times News Service, which prepared daily reports on topics of broad scientific interest for the *Times*. But I completely failed to see what an important "story" the work by Rowland and Molina would become, and never gave it the headlines and detailed coverage that, looking back from the perspective of 1987, it so obviously deserved. Nor did my colleagues and rivals in the United Kingdom. It was in the United States that the story began to make waves—but even there, it only hit the national headlines a few months later, when other teams published calculations confirming the reality of the threat uncovered by the Irvine researchers.

THE BANDWAGON ROLLS

Things began moving in September, when Rowland gave a presentation of his work with Molina to a meeting of the American Chemical Society, held in Atlantic City. This received wide coverage in newspapers across the country, but in a fairly low-key fashion compared with what was to follow. On September 26, 1974, the CFC/ozone story made the front page of the *New York Times*, in a story by Walter Sullivan describing calculations carried out by Mike McElroy's group at Harvard. Rowland and Molina were mentioned in passing. The next day, in the September 27 issue of *Science*, there was a paper from Stolarski and Cicerone, at Michigan, in which they presented *their* calculations of the impact of CFCs on stratospheric ozone. The coincidence of the timing of Sullivan's report and the appearance of their own paper in *Science*—if it was a coincidence—did nothing to make the Michigan team any happier about the Harvard group, whose own formal scientific paper, describing the work they had leaked to Sullivan in September, was not even received by *Science* until three days after the *Times* story appeared, and was not published until February 1975.

But if some of the scientists involved began to get hot under the collar about what they regarded as the inappropriate publicity-seeking of some of their peers (and it is only fair to mention that although *Nature* hardly ranks with the front page of the *New York Times* for publicity value, the work by Stolarski and Cicerone was alluded to in the *Nature* commentary in June, three months before it was published officially), that was nothing to the reaction of industry. By the end of 1974, the story had been splashed across the print media and had made national TV. Chemical giants involved in the manufacture of CFCs were quick to respond, questioning the accuracy of the claims being made not just by Rowland and Molina but by the Harvard and Michigan groups as well, and trying to make the case that the CFC industry was too big a contributor to employment and the economy to be put at risk on the basis of a few calculations made by a bunch of academic scientists.

The spray-can war ran through 1975 and into 1976, and has been documented in meticulous detail by Dotto and Schiff in their fascinating book, written just after the issue came to a head with the first legislation designed to protect the Earth's environment from damage caused by CFCs. The line taken by industry throughout the debate was that the projections made by Rowland, Molina, and others were made on the basis of "just a theory," and had not been proved by observations of the real atmosphere. It would be better to wait for a few years, and gather data, the argument ran, than to throw people out of work and jeopardize a billion-dollar industry for the sake of a few speculations.

On the other side of the fence, scientists (headed by Rowland, who became more and more of a political animal as the debate developed, and by Ralph Cicerone) argued that spray cans, in particular, were a luxury that we could do without, and that an immediate ban on the use of CFCs as aerosol propellants was called for. Other substances could, after all, be used as propellants, even if they weren't quite as well suited to the task as CFCs. And the unusual stability of CFCs in the troposphere made the "wait and see" approach untenable—by the time we could actually measure the depletion of ozone caused by these compounds, there would be so many CFC molecules going around that the effects would continue to build up for decades, even if production and emissions ceased at once. (This point struck home with full force in the 1980s, when the hole over Antarctica was discovered.) The United States, argued the environmental lobby, had to take a lead in controlling the release of CFCs, since in the mid-1970s it was by far the leading country in both the manufacture and the release of the chemicals. Then, arguing from a position of moral strength, America could, the lobbyists hoped, take a lead in persuading other countries to follow suit.

These two authors were ideally placed to tell the tale of the furious debate between the two opposed camps in the 1970s. Dotto, a journalist based in Toronto, had covered the ozone "story" almost from the beginning, and in February 1974 she had caused something of a panic at NASA headquarters in Washington with her questions concerning the problem of chlorine from the space shuttle rockets. At the time, the problem was still supposed to be a secret shared only by the NASA scientists themselves. Schiff, a professor of chemistry at York University, in Toronto, was the first person to measure the speed of the reaction between nitric oxide and ozone, and was the editor of the special volume of the *Canadian Journal of Chemistry* that reported the proceedings of the Kyoto meeting—plus those little extras from the Harvard and Michigan teams.

As expert observers from the scientific and press camps, both involved in the ozone debate of the mid-1970s, Dotto and Schiff describe the events of late 1974 and most of 1975 as "the Incredible Stratospheric Travelling Road Show and Debating Society," putting on performances in Washington, D.C., and also any state capitals where the local legislatures requested an appearance. But nothing new emerged from the debates. Part of the "wait and see" approach requested by industry rested upon their case that a $5 million research program was being undertaken, by industry itself, and would be complete in "only" two or three years. Rowland, in particular, dismissed this suggestion by pointing out that the U.S. government had already spent far more on the Climatic Impact Assessment Program, and there was no need to wait to cover the same ground again, less adequately.

The tone of much of the debate can be assessed from one example cited by the Toronto team. An article in the trade journal *Aerosol Age* commented on the fact that one of the public officials at one of the many hearings had fair skin and red hair. Fair-skinned, red-haired people are, of course, more prone to sunburn and skin cancer than are dark people, and the implication of the report was that such individuals were attempting to foist their minority views on the rest of the population.

Scientists were not immune from the backbiting, either. The American chemical manufacturers had been delighted, a little before the stratospheric roadshow got rolling, to find a British scientist, Richard Scorer, prepared to denounce the whole CIAP study as "pompous claptrap." Dotto and Schiff tell how Scorer was duly flown over to the United States, where he traveled across the continent, spreading the message that the idea of a link between CFCs and ozone depletion was "utter nonsense."

Only more research could provide the ammunition

needed to settle the war. In the early part of 1975, NASA made its ultimately successful bid to be the lead agency on this research, and began a newly coordinated series of observations of the stratosphere. As early as December 1974, Congressmen Paul Rogers of Florida, and Marvin Esch of Michigan, introduced a bill calling on the NAS (National Academy of Sciences) to study the problem and authorizing the Environmental Protection Agency (EPA) to ban CFCs if necessary. Hearings began, but the session of Congress finished a few days later, and the bill died with it. Further bills were introduced in the next session of Congress, in 1975, and a committee known as IMOS (a partial acronym for a tortuous name that included the words Inadvertent Modification of the Stratosphere) was set up. By June 1975, IMOS reported that there was "legitimate cause for concern." By then, however, the NAS was carrying out a more detailed study of CFCs and their likely effect on the stratosphere, and everyone was urged to hold their fire until the NAS report appeared. If the NAS study came out as expected, said IMOS, regulations could come in early in 1978. The committee recommended that spray cans that contained CFCs should be labeled so that the public knew which was which, and so that environmentally innocent spray cans, using different propellants, did not suffer from the consumer backlash against the can that was then building up. Industry and public alike took this as a verdict of "guilty until proven innocent," ensuring some ferocious propaganda activity in the months leading up to the NAS report. To anyone without a vested interest in the manufacture of CFCs, the verdict seemed (and still seems) reasonable enough— just a natural extension of the principle by which new drugs are not field-tested by letting consumers take them and watching to see if any of them drop dead, but are exhaustively tested for harmful effects first, on the assumption that until they are proved good for you they must be bad. But the industry didn't see it that way, and continued to fight its corner while waiting for the NAS panel to report.

The NAS study group had held its first meeting in April 1975 and was originally charged with reporting back by the beginning of April 1976. Harold Schiff, of York University, Toronto, was a member of the panel, and his book with Lydia Dotto (see bibliography, p. 183) is particularly insightful on the trials and tribulations of this period of scientific investigation being conducted in the full glare of public attention. For various reasons, the deliberations of the panel were extended. Other chemicals, notably chlorine nitrate, were brought into the discussion, and their effects had to be calculated. In addition, a new problem was raised by Paul Crutzen, who realized that, by changing the balance of heating in the atmosphere, destruction of ozone in the stratosphere would alter the climate of our planet (Crutzen has had an uncanny knack of identifying new problems linked to the depletion of ozone in the stratosphere; this one is now particularly chilling in light of changes currently going on in the Southern Hemisphere). The NAS report actually appeared in September 1976, after what seemed to the protagonists at the time to have been an unconscionable delay. From the perspective afforded by looking back over a decade later, in spite of all the huffing and puffing of the propaganda war, it seems that the scientific and political communities acted with commendable swiftness, produced a good assessment of the true nature of the problem, and acted promptly to take steps to alleviate it. Unfortunately, those steps proved too little, too late.

COMING UP-TO-DATE

On the basis of the NAS report, action was taken in the United States to limit the release of CFCs into the environment. Later improved calculations, using better chemistry and better computer models, have fully justified this action. The NAS report concluded that even if the release of CFCs were held to 1973 levels, there would, in the long term, be a reduction of between 6 and 7.5 percent in the concentration of ozone in the stratosphere, leading to an increase of 12 to 15 percent in the amount of ultraviolet radiation reaching the surface of the Earth. In May 1977, a joint statement issued by the Food and Drug Administration (FDA), the EPA, and the Consumer Product Safety Commission (CPSC) set the timetable for phasing out CFCs in spray cans, and in March 1978 the necessary regulations were issued. Under this legislation, manufacture of CFCs for aerosol propellants in the United States was banned in October 1978. Two months later, companies had to cease using existing supplies of CFC propellants in the manufacture of spray cans, and in April 1979 it became illegal to ship spray cans containing CFC propellants from one state to another. Minor loopholes in the law allowed the use of CFCs as the *active* ingredient in sprays, for example as cleansers in the electronics industry, and "essential" uses, including some medical applications such as sprays designed to apply painkillers without touching damaged skin. Although by then the United States was responsible for just under half of the total world emissions of CFCs each year, and a decreasing proportion had been going into spray cans since the scare broke in 1973, this was still a significant step in terms of protection of the global environment, and the overall release of CFCs worldwide fell for a few years as a result. In the 1980s, however, as other uses of CFCs continued to grow, and as other countries continued to use CFCs as propellants in spray cans, the total emissions began to rise once again. In 1978, the Chemical Manufacturers Association started a network of monitoring stations around the world, building from Lovelock's pioneering work, to monitor the content of CFCs in the atmosphere. The manufacturers hoped to find evidence that these compounds were in fact being destroyed in the troposphere and were not reaching the ozone layer in the amounts predicted. But they were disappointed. The monitoring program, called the Atmospheric Lifetime Experiment, or ALE, shows that the concentrations of F-11 and F-12 in the atmosphere are now about 230 parts per trillion and 400 parts per trillion, respectively. ALE has since been superseded by the Global Atmospheric Gases Experiment (GAGE), which is funded chiefly by NASA and the National Oceanographic and Atmospheric Administration with a contribution from the Chemical Manufacturers Association, and runs four automated observing stations, in Oregon, Barbados, Samoa, and Tasmania. The measurements still show, exactly as Lovelock noticed in the early 1970s, that essentially all the CFCs released into the environment are still in the atmosphere. And the concentrations are rising at a rate of about 5 percent a year.

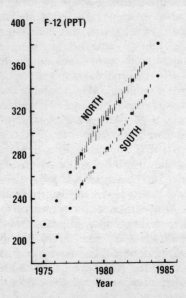

The concentrations still sound small. But in 1987, Sherry Rowland estimated that a single atom of chlorine released into the stratosphere would destroy 100,000 molecules of ozone before itself getting locked up in some less reactive form (perhaps as Cl_2) and falling out into the troposphere. At present rates of release, F-11 and F-12 are being put into the atmosphere six times faster than they are being destroyed by ultraviolet in the stratosphere, and that is why the concentration of these substances in both the troposphere and the stratosphere is increasing. Indeed, the concentrations in the atmosphere still increased between 1974 and 1980, when emissions actually fell slightly—confirmation of the long lifetime of the compounds in the atmosphere. Because only one-sixth of the CFCs entering the environment are being destroyed, cutting back present emissions to just one-sixth (15 percent) of their present levels would be necessary to stop the *present* concentration in the atmosphere from increasing—and the present concentration is already seriously damaging the ozone layer over Antarctica. Reducing the concentration of CFCs in the air would require cutting back even further on emissions, preferably all the way to zero. But even that would leave CFCs floating around in significant quantities until the second half of the twenty-first century. Attempts to tackle the problem in 1987 aimed at cutting emissions to about 85 percent of present levels in the short term—ludicrously inadequate if the buildup of CFCs is to be halted.

Following the success of initial legislation on spray-can propellants, in 1980 the Environmental Protection Agency outlined proposals for limiting overall CFC production in the United States, including other uses such as refrigeration, to then-current levels. But the change of administration in 1981 effectively killed off those plans—the environment had been a political issue which, by and large, fitted the philosophy of the Carter administration, but the same could not be said of the Reagan administration, operating with a president who, notoriously, had once said to a lobbier concerned about the destruction of California's forests, "If you've seen one redwood, you've seen 'em all." But while the political climate shifted against the environmental lobby in the United States, in the 1980s a long, slow process of international discussions under the auspices of the United Nations Environment Program (UNEP) eventually led to an agreement known as the Vienna Convention for the Protection of the Ozone Layer, signed in March 1985 and brought into force by the badly timed Montreal meeting in 1987.

Research carried out for the Vienna convention provides the latest, and best, bench mark against which to assess the risks to the stratosphere. Modelers from different countries met in Würzburg, West Germany, in April 1987 and concluded that even an immediate, worldwide halt to the growth in release of CFCs would still leave a depletion of the ozone concentration of the stratosphere worldwide of 1 percent by the year 2050. With growth of CFC emissions at 3 percent a year, the 1 percent decline in ozone concentrations occurs by the year 2000, and the decline reaches 4 percent by 2040. But how reliable are the models? Data from an experiment on board the *Nimbus* 7 satellite suggest that ozone in northern latitudes has recently been disappearing four to six times faster than the models imply; the measurements suggest that total ozone is already down by some 3 percent. And all of this paled into insignificance with the discoveries made in Antarctica by the Punta Arenas expedition in the Southern Hemisphere in the spring of 1987. *None* of the models had even hinted at the kind of depletion of ozone over Antarctica that is now being seen every year.

The environmental lobby won the spray-can war in the United States in the 1970s. But then the lobbyists found that this was not the whole war at all, but merely the first battle in a much bigger campaign—a campaign

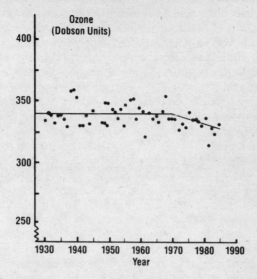

that still involves the use of CFCs in spray cans in other countries, but which now also involves chemical fertilizers, pollution from car exhausts, CFCs and other chlorine-bearing compounds that have escaped regulation so far, plus natural influences such as volcanic eruptions. By the time the Antarctic ozone hole was discovered, it seemed that just about everything going into the atmosphere would be likely to disrupt the natural balance of ozone in the stratosphere.

CHAPTER FOUR

OZONE EATERS AND THE BIOSPHERE

Although the SST problem never really became a serious threat to the ozone layer in the 1970s, simply because so few SSTs ever left the ground, the question of the relationship between NO_x and the stratosphere continued to provide environmental chemists with food for thought. Nitrogen oxides occur naturally in the atmosphere, and reach the stratosphere, where they are involved in the chemical balancing act that maintains a layer of ozone above our heads. The importance of NO_x in helping to maintain this dynamic equilibrium, in which ozone is constantly being destroyed by some photochemical processes but constantly being replenished by others, was appreciated only in the late 1960s. Before then, chemists had tried to balance the books without involving NO_x, and their calculations indicated that twice as much ozone was being produced as was being destroyed—clear nonsense, since measurements showed that the concentration of ozone in the stratosphere was not increasing dramatically. It was Paul

Crutzen who pointed out that NO_x, occurring naturally in the environment, would provide an important "sink" for ozone in the stratosphere. He managed to balance the chemical books in a paper published in 1970. This led directly to his interest in the SST debate and his continuing participation in the work on ozone, up to and including the present attempts to understand the hole over Antarctica.

Just because NO_x, unlike CFCs, is a natural part of the environment does not mean that it is "safe," however, or that it cannot be disturbed by human activities—as the SST and space shuttle examples highlighted. By 1974, when the first shots in the spray-can war were being fired, Crutzen had also identified another possible source of NO_x pollution, which he mentioned in a paper summarizing various possible causes, both natural and due to human activities, that might cause variations in the concentration of ozone in the stratosphere. In some ways, this new suggestion was even more alarming than the CFC threat, since it now seemed that chemical fertilizers being used on farmland could significantly increase the rate of destruction of ozone in the stratosphere. Maybe we could do without spray cans, but could we do without fertilizers in a world with a rapidly growing population?

The latest calculations suggest that any impact from fertilizer use on the stratosphere is likely to be relatively small, compared with some other pollutant effects, and slow to take off—but remember how several "relatively small" effects can add up to something to worry about. Understanding how this possible threat arises, however, is especially relevant to the whole debate about the relationship between humankind and the environment, since it brings out, more clearly than any other aspect of the ozone debate, just how interdependent the physical environment and the living organisms of our planet really are. Look at the nitrogen cycle at work, and you see Gaia come to life.

CYCLES OF LIFE

There are 92 natural occurring chemical elements found on Earth, but only 27 of these elements are essential for life, and most of the molecules of living things are built up from surprisingly few of these building blocks. The most important element in the molecules of living things—organic matter—is carbon, which has an unusual ability to combine with up to four other atoms, including carbon atoms that are themselves linked to other atoms, and so on, to form complex molecules. Carbon is so important to life that the study of carbon compounds is, indeed, known as organic chemistry. Leaving aside water, which makes up just over three-quarters of the weight of the human body, more than half of the rest (the dry weight) of your body is carbon. A quarter of the dry weight is oxygen, and about 10 percent is nitrogen.

Nitrogen is a key ingredient of the many different kinds of protein that make up a living body. It occurs most commonly in a unit that is derived from ammonia, NH_3. By giving up one of its hydrogen atoms, the nitrogen atom in this molecule can latch on to a carbon atom, to form an amine group, CNH_2. Such a group does not float around freely in your body, or anywhere else, since the carbon atom itself will be joined to up to three other atoms (which themselves may be joined to yet other atoms, and so on) as part of a much more complex molecule. But the amine group has characteristic chemical properties, even as a subunit of a larger molecule, and it gives its name to one class of organic molecules, the amino acids, which are essential to life.

All amino acids contain several atoms of carbon and hydrogen, a couple of oxygen atoms, and at least one amine group, arranged in different ways. Proteins are made of chains of amino acids stuck together, and just twenty different types of amino acid are required to manufacture all the proteins in the human body. The way amino acids join together to make proteins depends on the affinity carbon and nitrogen atoms have for each other. When two amino acids join, the amine group in one amino acid gives up another of its hydrogen atoms, and a carbon atom in the other amino acid releases an OH group. The H and OH combine to form water, H_2O, and the two amino acids join through a carbon-nitrogen bond. Carbon-nitrogen bonds form the essential links that hold proteins together. As if that were not an important enough role to play in life processes, nitrogen atoms are also important constituents of nucleic acids, the DNA and RNA molecules that carry the genetic code, immortalized as the "double helix."

So living things need nitrogen. Where do they get it? Since so much of the atmosphere of our planet is free nitrogen, you might think it would be easy. But almost all atmospheric nitrogen is in the form of diatomic molecules, N_2, which are very stable and very difficult to split apart. Unless the molecules are split apart into individual atoms, which takes energy, the nitrogen atoms are not available to react with other substances. The fact that amino acids are so important to life provides a clue that early forms of life on Earth obtained their nitrogen from ammonia itself. Just how much ammonia may have been around in the early atmosphere of the Earth is still a matter of debate, but there was certainly more than there is today, and it would have formed an ingredient of the primordial soup. As life spread, however, the supply of ammonia must have become exhausted, and some living things had to "learn" how to extract nitrogen from the air itself and to incorporate it into living molecules—a process known as *nitrogen fixation*, which basically involves using atmospheric nitrogen to make ammonia.

A plant that cannot fix nitrogen is like a thirsty man

on a life raft in the middle of the ocean. He is surrounded by water and cannot drink it; the plant is
immersed in nitrogen and cannot use it. Animals do not
have this problem, since they obtain their amino acids
by eating plants, or by eating other animals that have
themselves eaten plants. Even most plants do not fix
nitrogen directly for themselves, but extract it from the
soil in the form of nitrates. But the bottom line is that all
life on Earth depends on some life forms, somewhere,
that do the job of fixing nitrogen out of the atmosphere,
and are responsible for the presence of those nitrates in
the soil in the first place.

The pressure on life to find a way to fix nitrogen
must have been very strong, very early in the history of
the Earth. There are bacteria known today that obtain
their energy only through fermentation, the more primitive process that predates photosynthesis, but which
can still carry out the more complicated chemical trick
of nitrogen fixation. Their ancestors, clearly, never came
under pressure to develop photosynthesis, but they did
need nitrogen fixation in order to survive. Just how
nitrogen is fixed by biological organisms, including these
presumably primitive forms of bacteria, is still something of a mystery. Nitrogen-fixing organisms use energy to split water molecules apart, releasing hydrogen,
which they then combine with nitrogen to make ammonia. The trick requires a lot of energy, and it takes place
with the aid of a catalyst, an enzyme known as *nitrogenase*,
which somehow encourages the chemical reactions. Intense, and so far unsuccessful, efforts have been made
to understand the chemistry involved and to reproduce
it; success in these endeavors would provide a means of
fixing nitrogen more or less at will and give a great
boost for agriculture. But perhaps, as we shall see, that
would be a mixed blessing.

The remarkable properties of nitrogenase can be
seen by comparing the effectiveness of this enzyme
with other processes that take nitrogen out of the air

and turn it into molecules that can be used by plants. Lightning flashes, which heat the air in their path to about 18,000 degrees F, provide energy that breaks up some nitrogen molecules into atoms and encourages the formation of nitric acid (later converted into nitrates) as they react with oxygen and water in the air. Industrial processes for fixing nitrogen involve reactions under high pressure and at high temperature in sealed vessels. Bacteria do the trick routinely, under everyday conditions of temperature and pressure. Yet it would take 20,000 of these bacteria, side by side, to span a distance of a little over a third of an inch; and it has been estimated that the total amount of nitrogenase in the world, on which all life depends, is no more than several pounds.

Bacteria that fix nitrogen occur throughout the living world. Rainwater that falls on a tree contains more dissolved nitrogen at the top of the tree than at the bottom, because organisms that can fix nitrogen* live on the leaves and branches of the tree, and have done their work while the water has trickled over them. But most nitrogen is fixed by bacteria that live in a very close, symbiotic relationship with certain plants. These are the leguminous plants, such as peas, beans, clover, soybeans, and peanuts. The bacteria are known as rhizobia, and they live either in or near the roots of the plants. The environment provided by the plant suits the bacteria and gives them a good home; the nitrogen compounds provided by the bacteria not only benefit the host plant, but escape into the soil and enrich it. This is the origin of the practice of crop rotation, which farmers invented long before they knew anything about nitrogen or bacteria. Soil that has been drained of nitrogen compounds by other crops, and would otherwise

---

*Not just bacteria; some other "primitive" forms, such as algae and lichen, can also do the trick. But bacteria play the key role.

give only poor yields as a result, can be revived by planting it with one of the leguminous crops, as part of the cycle of crop rotation. One of the aims of plant biologists today is to find a way either of persuading rhizobia to take up home in the roots of grain plants, or to use genetic engineering techniques to introduce genes for nitrogenase itself into the cells of the grains.

Today, plants do not have to take up the nitrogen they require in the form of ammonia. As the oxygen atmosphere of the Earth developed, nitrates, compounds that contain nitrogen and oxygen linked with other elements, became more common in the soil, partly because of the effects of lightning on the atmosphere, but chiefly because ammonia produced by nitrogen-fixing bacteria itself reacts with oxygen, either directly from the air or in further biological processes leading to the production of nitrates. Plants take up nitrates and use them to produce ammonia, with carbon dioxide being released as a byproduct.

All this may seem a far cry from the ozone layer in the stratosphere. But at this point another kind of bacteria get in on the act. Because plants use nitrates, there is not usually very much nitrate around in the soil. But there is some, including nitrates derived from the remains of once-living organisms, and living things will generally find a way to make use of any resource that is available. Some bacteria that usually get their energy by respiration (taking up oxygen from the air and "burning" it with carbon just as we do) have also developed the ability to get their oxygen from nitrates. This represents impressive versatility, but the oxygen in nitrates is not so freely available as oxygen in the air, so nitrate respiration is something of a last resort for these "denitrifying" bacteria. If there is no free oxygen at all available, in water below the surface of the ground or somewhere else cut off from the air, they will use all the oxygen in the nitrates, releasing nitrogen back into the environment as stable diatomic molecules of N_2. If, however, there is a little free oxygen in their environment, but not enough to live on, they take just what they need from the nitrates to make up the balance. In this case, the waste product they release still contains some oxygen. It is nitrous oxide, N_2O, also known as laughing gas.

At this point, the biological cycle is complete. Nitrogen has been cycled back into the atmosphere and can be fixed once again and used by future generations of living things (the energy that keeps the cycle going comes ultimately, of course, from sunlight). Along the way, just a little nitrous oxide has been produced. And at this point biology has an impact on ozone.

LAUGHING GAS IS NOT SO FUNNY

Nitrous oxide has anesthetic properties and in small doses produces symptoms like those of drunkenness, which gives it its popular name. But apart from this interesting property, it is very unreactive. There are no known naturally occuring chemical reactions that destroy it in the troposphere, or that tie it up in other chemical forms, and once released it drifts around and accumulates, eventually finding its way up into the stratosphere. The story sounds familiar, and so are the consequences. In the stratosphere, ultraviolet radiation promotes reactions that break up nitrous oxide and produce other forms of NO_x, especially NO, which react with ozone. This is a natural process that, as we have seen, helps to maintain the present balance of ozone in the stratosphere. The feedback with life is doubly fascinating, since the oxygen in the air, from which ozone derives, is itself produced by living things. If Lovelock's Gaia hypothesis is correct, the amount of N_2O, and therefore of NO, being produced naturally will have struck a balance that maintains the concentration of ozone in the stratosphere at the right amount to shield the surface of the Earth from damaging ultraviolet radiation, while allowing through just enough radiation to maintain conditions suitable for life. The problem that Crutzen identified in 1974 is that by adding nitrate fertilizers to the soil (not just in farmland but also in our parks and, especially in America, golf courses, which eat up 10 percent of fertilizers used in the United States) we are providing the raw material for denitrifying bacteria to feast on, and are thereby adding to the burden of N_2O in the troposphere and NO in the stratosphere.

The issue clearly demonstrates the potential hazards of unwitting interference with the environment, even when the motives—increasing food production—are good. But it is very difficult to quantify this particular threat to the ozone layer. The amount of NO reaching the stratosphere depends on the amount of N_2O produced by the denitrifying bacteria, and it is by no means obvious that doubling the amount of nitrates, say, would double their activity. They do the denitrifying trick only when they are short of oxygen, especially in wet soils, and even then most of the time they are so short of oxygen that they take it all from the nitrates, releasing mostly harmless nitrogen gas. Then there is the question of how quickly nitrates added to the soil are processed by bacteria. The whole point of adding such fertilizers to the soil is to encourage the growth of crop plants, and these get eaten and become part of the biological cycle. Excess nitrates, washed away from the fields, may encourage the growth of trees in the forests next door, or of microorganisms in the rivers, lakes, and seas. It might be a very long time indeed before much of the nitrogen is available to the denitrifying bacteria, even if they want, or need, to use it. But the figures for human production of nitrates are alarming.

Natural processes, it has been estimated, fix about 300 million tons of nitrogen a year. In the mid-1970s, when Crutzen mentioned the problem, human activities were adding about 15 percent to this. Fertilizer use has been growing rapidly since then, in spite of the effect of energy price increases (the manufacture of nitrate fertilizers requires a great deal of energy), and some estimates suggest that we will be adding as much nitrate to the soil as all natural processes combined by the early years of the twenty-first century. That will represent such a dramatic change in the natural balance that is it virtually impossible to predict the consequences, not just for the ozone layer but for other components of the ecosystem.

Nitrous oxide is also being added to the atmosphere by combustion, every time coal or oil is burned in the air. The heat of the fire breaks down some of the nitrogen molecules in the atmosphere, and a few of these then combine with oxygen to make N_2O. This nonbiological nitrous oxide follows exactly the same atmospheric cycle as the laughing gas released by denitrification. Estimates of the combined effects of fertilizers and NO_x from combustion on stratospheric ozone vary widely, and are little more than educated guesses. However, there are now measurements of the amount of N_2O in the troposphere, which was 304 parts per billion in 1984 and is rising at a rate of about 0.7 parts per billion (that is, one-quarter of 1 percent) per year. A small contribution to the burden of nitrous oxide in the troposphere (and therefore to the burden of NO_x in the stratosphere) also comes from spray cans. Several of my friends, who thought they were doing the right thing by refusing to buy spray cans containing CFCs, have been more than a little upset when I have pointed out to them the potential hazards from nitrous oxide, which is also used as a propellant, most visibly in spray cans of whipped cream. Of course, nobody "needs" spray-on whipped cream; but it is particularly upsetting to someone who has read the label carefully and happily bought the item secure in the knowledge that it contains no CFCs to learn that N_2O is, possibly, just as bad.

Whatever the origins of the gas, just as in the case of CFCs, the long lifetime of N_2O (in this case, 150 years) in the troposphere means that the effects add up from year to year, and decade to decade, so the increase will exceed 1 percent over the 1984 baseline well before the year 2000. If the same proportion of "extra" NO gets into the stratosphere, then laughing gas clearly has to be considered in any discussion of exactly what we should cut down on, and when, to minimize the threat to ozone.

There is, however, no certainty that an increase of 1 or 2 percent in the release of nitrous oxide will add 1 or 2 percent to the burden of NO_x in the stratosphere. At present, although several hundred million tons of N_2O are being released into the troposphere each year (the estimates differ on the precise figure) only a few tens of millions of tons get transferred to the stratosphere (again, the estimates differ in detail). *Most* of the nitrous oxide, unlike the CFCs, is going somewhere else, and we don't know where. At first sight, that looks reassuring. But if that natural sink is disturbed by human activities, which seems all too likely given the way those activities are now impinging on the environment, or if the sink simply can't cope with the extra burden of N_2O that results from human activities, we might suddenly find a very large increase in the amount of N_2O moving up into the stratosphere. And, unfortunately, nitrous oxide is far from being the only additional factor, other than CFCs, that has to be taken into consideration.

DINOSAURS AND DOOMSDAY SCENARIOS

Some of the potential problems for stratospheric chemistry are beyond human control, although they do have relevance to an area of human activities that is beyond the control of most of us—the prospect of nuclear war. Is it possible, some scientists have asked, that the extinction of the dinosaurs, some 65 million years ago, was related to a catastrophic depletion of ozone in the stratosphere, caused either by the effects on the Earth of a nearby supernova explosion or by an outburst of solar activity at a time when the Earth's protecting magnetic field was weak?

Something certainly did strike down the dinosaurs, and many other species, and that "something" probably came from above, since fossil evidence shows that creatures living in the sea were largely unaffected by the catastrophe. Of course, paleontologists point out that the dinosaurs had been in decline for some time before this terminal event, but that indicates merely that other environmental changes may have left them vulnerable to a "last straw" effect. In recent years, the fashionable explanation for the death of the dinosaurs has been to invoke climatic changes linked with the impact of a large meteorite hitting the Earth, flinging dust high into the atmosphere. Ideas linked to changes in the ozone layer have gone out of fashion but are still as respectable as when they were put forward in the 1970s.

The two variations on the theme both operate through the same mechanism. Protons (hydrogen nuclei) that arrive at the Earth from space, as cosmic rays, interact with the upper atmosphere to release atoms of nitrogen, which then filter down through the mesosphere and stratosphere, forming molecules of NO_x and initiating the chain reactions that destroy ozone.

Such cosmic rays from space are always entering the Earth's atmosphere, but most of the time their effect is very small. This is partly because they do not usually arrive in very large numbers, and partly because they have an electric charge (a proton is simply a hydrogen atom with its electron knocked off), and charged particles cannot penetrate the Earth's magnetic field. The only place they might have a noticeable effect today is near the poles, where they are funneled by the magnetic lines of force; but there is no convincing evidence that they are involved in the production of the Antarctic ozone hole.

There are two ways to increase the effect of cosmic rays on the stratosphere: make the cosmic rays stronger, or make the Earth's magnetic field weaker—or both. Iosef Shklovski, a Soviet astronomer, and Martin Ruderman, in the United States, originally developed the first scenario, proposing that the explosion of a star in the neighborhood of the Solar System, a supernova, could produce such a flood of cosmic rays that 50 percent or more of the ozone layer was destroyed. If that happened today, it could certainly be as catastrophic for present life forms as the disaster 65 million years ago was for the dinosaurs. Severe sunburn, with skin blistering within ten minutes, and blindness would be among the immediate problems confronting people and animals. As plants withered in the ultraviolet glare, we would then be left with a longer-term problem of finding something to eat. The prospect is remote—astronomers calculate that there is a 1 in 100 chance of a supernova near enough to do the damage occurring in any 20-million-year interval. But then, catastrophes like the extinction of the dinosaurs are also rare events.

The related scenario links destruction of the ozone shield to changes in terrestrial magnetism and to the Sun's activity. It happens that the Earth's magnetic field, which is generated by swirling currents of magnetic material in its molten interior, itself varies. Sometimes it dies away entirely and then rebuilds in intensity, either in the same direction (with the north and south magnetic poles aligned as they were before) or in the opposite sense, with the magnetic poles reversed. Fossils show that such magnetic reversals are often associated with small-scale extinctions of species, though seldom on the scale of the death of the dinosaurs. However, the Earth's magnetic field was indeed variable at about the time the dinosaurs died out, as traces of magnetism in old rocks reveal.

Solar activity also varies, not only following a cycle of activity roughly 11 years long (the sunspot cycle) but also, occasionally, producing larger outbursts of flaring activity, which send streams of protons across space to the Earth. If the Sun produced an outburst of protons just at a time when the Earth's magnetic field was weak, they might penetrate the atmosphere and damage the ozone shield. One of the pioneers of this idea was the ubiquitous Paul Crutzen, working with Ivar Isaksen and George Reid. Their calculations, published in 1975, weren't just of interest to those studying the extinction of the dinosaurs. Even without the Earth's magnetic field being particularly weak, a large enough solar flare could do at least some damage to the stratosphere. It happened that there had been a particularly large burst of activity from the Sun in August 1972. In 1975, Crutzen and his colleagues calculated that, if their model was correct, such an outburst should have reduced the concentration of ozone over the North Pole by between 15 and 20 percent, because the solar protons would have been focused there by the Earth's magnetic field. Following these calculations, Donald Heath and Arlin Kreuger, of NASA, dug out some old data obtained by the weather satellite *Nimbus 4* but never previously analyzed in the right way to show ozone fluctuation. They found that the satellite had observed a decrease in north polar ozone of 16 percent following the solar flare of 1972.

This was the most dramatic short-term change in ozone content of the stratosphere observed before the discovery of the Antarctic hole. Just what the effect over Antarctica might be if a similar solar storm erupted while the hole is at its greatest seasonal extent, nobody has been able to calculate. Although the idea of a link between ozone changes and the death of the dinosaurs is now unfashionable, it has important ramifications today, and the events of 1972 confirmed the accuracy of the models used to calculate the ozone changes.

Such a confirmation of the accuracy of the models helps us to have faith in the calculations of other influences on ozone, including the effect of CFCs. Rational people shouldn't need any reminding that nuclear war would be a bad thing, but just how bad a thing it might be was also highlighted in the mid-1970s, after John Hampson, who had done some of the pioneering work on the role of HO_x in the stratosphere, became concerned about the effects of NO_x from nuclear explosions. After Hampson raised the issue, in a paper published in *Nature* in 1974, a National Academy of Sciences workshop held in January 1975 reached the conclusion that a war involving the explosion of half the world's 1974 stockpile of nuclear weapons—10,000 megatons—would reduce the concentration of ozone over the Northern Hemisphere (where most of the warheads exploded) by between 30 and 70 percent, and over the Southern Hemisphere by between 20 and 40 percent. These are very much the sort of figures implicated, by some studies, in the extinction of the dinosaurs, and could very well have a similar effect on the human species, among others.

There is no direct evidence that atmospheric nuclear explosions destroy stratospheric ozone, since nobody was making the necessary detailed measurements in the 1950s and early 1960s, when atmospheric testing was common. But the available overall measurements do show that the total ozone content of the stratosphere

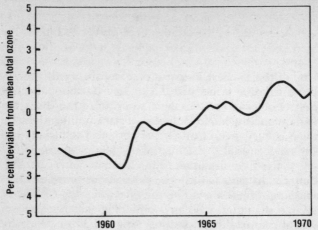

increased, in spite of some fluctuations, in the years following 1963, after atmospheric testing was banned by the major nuclear powers. This would be consistent with the atmosphere's recovering from the effects of all the nuclear tests that had gone before. Of course, the point is largely academic. Anyone crazy enough to start a nuclear war probably won't be dissuaded by the thought of the damage it might do to the ozone layer, any more than by the prospect of climatic changes. (The threat of a "nuclear winter" has now been downgraded by improved calculations to a "nuclear fall," but would still be sufficiently severe to have a major effect in reducing crop yields even in regions of the globe that escaped the nuclear warheads themselves.) But this work, like the studies of possible causes of the death of the dinosaurs, does serve as a reminder that the ozone shield is not indestructible and certainly can be damaged both by natural events and by human activities. Other candidates for disaster are less apocalyptic but are more likely to happen in the immediate future—except for one spinoff from the chlorine debate that also involves the kind of lunacy represented by the idea of nuclear war.

LITTLE THINGS MAY MEAN A LOT

One of the craziest items to emerge during the some-times frenzied debate in the mid-1970s about the im-pact of chloroflurocarbons on the stratosphere was the suggestion, by Mike McElroy, that bromine might be used as a weapon of war, to bring about artificially the kind of conditions that, perhaps, killed off the dino-saurs. Bromine is in the same chemical family as chlo-rine, the halogens, and shares many of its properties. If anything, it reacts even more effectively with ozone. In 1975, it was quite reasonable of McElroy to draw atten-tion to the possible hazard to the ozone layer posed by the widespread use of methyl bromide in agriculture, as a fumigant against insects and rodents, both in food and tobacco. Although methyl bromide does not have the unusual stability of CFCs in the troposphere, and is broken down to some extent before reaching the strato-sphere, it certainly seems plausible that there might be a small additional effect on ozone from this source. And, after all, all those small effects add up, perhaps to the point where an accumulation of little things makes a significant hazard. In the same year, Steve Wofsy and his colleagues pointed to another potential contribu-tion, from a family of chemicals much more closely related to CFCs, called *brominated chlorocarbons*. These are used in firefighting. Neither source of bromine is anywhere near the CFC league as a threat to ozone. But McElroy hit the headlines by suggesting that bro-mine deliberately released into the stratosphere could be used as a weapon, eating a huge hole in the ozone layer over enemy territory, incapacitating unprotected people and destroying crops. The fact that the effect, if real, would soon spread around the world and cause as much damage to the nation that set off the bromine "bomb," making it very much a last-resort, suicide weapon, seemed only to whet the appetites of writers for publications such as the *National Enquirer*. The resulting publicity infuriated many of McElroy's colleagues, who felt that it threw a smokescreen over the much more serious debate about CFCs. The "doomsday weapon" scenario can be ignored. But that doesn't mean that we shouldn't be aware that human activities are putting bromine into the atmosphere, and that this may add to the depletion of stratospheric ozone.

What else could be adding to that depletion? There are natural sources of chlorine, and these should certainly be taken into account. Volcanic eruptions occasionally inject large amounts of chlorine compounds into the stratosphere, and these can produce a dramatic, if short lived, impact. In the year following the eruption of El Chichón, in 1982, observations made at a monitoring station in Arosa, Switzerland, showed the lowest measure of annual ozone overhead ever recorded. The largest more or less steady natural source of atmospheric chlorine is, however, in the form of methyl chloride (known also as *chloromethane*). A little of this comes from industrial processes, but a great deal seems to originate from burning plant material. Since this includes both natural forest fires and the fires associated with slash-and-burn agriculture, there is some debate about the extent to which the present burden of methyl chloride in the atmosphere (a few parts per billion) is "natural" and how much is due to human activities. Whatever its origins, about 90 percent of methyl chloride is removed from the troposphere by chemical reactions, and only about 10 percent, or less, reaches the stratosphere. Even so, calculations made in the mid-1970s suggest that at that time methyl chloride may have been as effective at destroying ozone as CFCs were.

Like the natural background of NO_x resulting from denitrification, this is part of the natural cycle that maintains the concentration of ozone in the stratosphere; what matters is that human activities may tilt the balance and change the rate at which ozone is being destroyed. Nobody has any good estimate of how the methyl chloride balance might tilt in the next few decades.

Human influences are more clearly implicated in the buildup of a similarly named compound, methyl chloroform (known also as *trichloroethane*) in the atmosphere. There is a fine irony here. Trichloroethylene, a similar compound to methyl chloroform, has been widely used as a degreasing fluid, for cleaning metal surfaces in particular, and also in the dry-cleaning industry. This compound breaks down very quickly in the atmosphere and so poses no threat to the stratosphere. But because it reacts near the ground, it contributes to the reactions that produce photochemical smog. Therefore, the Environmental Protection Agency, in its wisdom, decided to restrict the use of trichloroethylene in the United States and recommended the use of methyl cloroform instead. This does not contribute to the smog problem because—you guessed—it reacts very slowly in the troposphere. Which means, of course, that significant quantities reach the stratosphere, where they are broken down by ultraviolet radiation, releasing chlorine atoms that can become involved in scavenging ozone. By trying to solve one problem, the EPA has exacerbated another. The use of methyl chloroform is now growing quite rapidly, at about 7 percent a year, and the concentration in the troposphere in 1987 was about 130 parts per trillion. Fortunately, it has a lifetime of only a little over 6 years, so it poses less of a threat to the ozone layer than CFCs do; but some calculations suggest that it may still contribute a 1 or 2 percent overall reduction in ozone concentrations of the stratosphere by the middle of the next century.

Mention of dry-cleaning fluids still makes many people think of carbon tetrachloride, the archetypal dry-cleaning agent. In fact, the use of carbon tetrachloride in Europe and North America has been restricted for some time, because of its toxic properties. It certainly has the potential to eat ozone, since it contains chlorine and has a lifetime of about 50 years in the atmosphere; significant amounts do reach the stratosphere. In the 1970s, it looked as if this particular contribution to the problem might disappear, since the amount of carbon tetrachloride in the environment was declining slightly. But since then the use of carbon tetrachloride has crept up again, and the atmospheric concentration is now growing at about 1 percent a year, from the 1987 level of 125 parts per trillion. This increase is partly because Third World countries have developed industrially, but it is due also to growth in the developed nations. Carbon tetrachloride is now used in fire extinguishers and, like methyl bromide, as a fumigant. It is also manufactured as an intermediate step in the production of dichlorodifluoromethane (CCl_2F_2), a compound we have already met, which is used as a refrigerant and as a propellant in spray cans, and is sometimes known as F-12.

Another kind of problem is posed by the buildup of methane in the atmosphere. Analysis of bubbles of air trapped in the ice of glaciers shows that the methane content of the atmosphere took off from a level of 700 parts per billion (where it had been for at least a thousand years) during the eighteenth century. It is now about 1,650 parts per billion and is increasing at a rate between 1 and 2 percent a year. Almost certainly, the increase in methane is linked with the worldwide development of agriculture and the explosive growth of human population. Methane is manufactured by bacteria in places where oxygen is in short supply—in swamps (which is why it is known as *marsh gas*), in the guts of animals, and in termite mounds. As human population has grown, so has the population of cattle to feed the people—and the rear ends of cattle are a notorious source of methane. A bigger contribution comes from rice paddies, which are, in effect, artificial swamps.

Whatever its origins, methane is building up in the stratosphere, especially in the upper levels of the troposphere. One of the effects this has on atmospheric chemistry is to *increase* the amount of ozone. Methane reacts with chlorine to produce hydrochloric acid (among other things), which falls out of the sky as acid rain. With less chlorine present, there is more ozone around the tropopause. The bad news is that this may have been masking the depletion at higher altitudes.

In 1984, the UN's Consultative Committee on the Ozone Layer (one of the bodies that provided input for the Vienna convention) reported that there had been a 3 percent depletion of ozone in the stratosphere since 1970. The bad news was that these measurements were based on looking upward through the whole atmosphere from the ground—total column measurements. Allowing for the methane effect, that 3 percent overall decline corresponded to a decrease of 14 percent in the high stratosphere, and a corresponding increase near the tropopause. At that rate, said the committee, by the year 2000 the total column would have decreased by only 5 percent, but the decrease at about 25 miles would be about 40 percent. Relatively good news if you are worried mainly about skin cancer; less good if you consider the climatic implications.

Such simplistic predictions may well be naïve. For one thing, they are based on the assumption that things will continue to change smoothly as the burden of CFCs and other ozone-eaters increases. For years, a few scientists have warned that the atmospheric systems may in fact respond in a nonlinear fashion. That is, they may change abruptly into a completely different state once some crucial threshold is reached. You can get the picture by imagining a naïve scientist watching a block of ice being slowly warmed from 25 degrees F. When the temperature has reached 30 degrees F, the scientist predicts, on the basis of the observations so far, that increasing the temperature by a further 5 degrees F will have no significant effect on the ice block. But as soon as the temperature rises above 32 degrees F, that forecast will be in ruins. Recent events over Antarctica suggest that something similar has happened there.

As if nonlinearity were not enough of a problem, there are complications caused by other effects of gases like methane (and, indeed, CFCs) on the environment of the Earth. Depletion of the ozone content of the stratosphere will change the heat balance of the Earth, allowing more radiation to penetrate to the ground and making the troposphere hotter while the stratosphere cools. Equally, anything else that changes the heat balance of the Earth will have a profound effect on the ozone layer, since the rates at which the chemical reactions involving ozone proceed depend on temperature. There is, clearly, the possibility of a feedback here, in which ozone depletion changes the temperature, and that causes further ozone depletion, and so on. But there is also another influence on global temperatures now at work.

Many gases being released into the atmosphere by human activities, including methane and CFCs, but most notably carbon dioxide, contribute to the greenhouse effect, which keeps the Earth warm. As these gases build up in the atmosphere, climatologists expect the troposphere to warm significantly over the next few decades, while the stratosphere cools. As weather patterns change, the greenhouse effect may well become a more significant environmental problem than the destruction of the ozone layer. Meanwhile, the cooling of the stratosphere may already have begun, and may be contributing to the development of the Antarctic hole—with CFCs, as the third-ranked contributors to the anthropogenic greenhouse effect, after carbon dioxide and methane, playing their part in yet another feedback loop.

CHAPTER FIVE

GREENHOUSE GASES

The greenhouse effect is an essential component of the web of interactions that makes the Earth a suitable home for life. The blanket of air around the globe not only traps heat that would otherwise escape out into space, it also distributes the heat more evenly than it would otherwise be distributed, from the sunlit, day side of the Earth to the dark, night side, and from the equator to the poles.

You can get some idea of just how important this is by looking at the Moon, which is essentially at the same distance from the Sun as the Earth is. On the airless Moon, however, the temperature rises to the boiling point of water, 212 degrees F, under the full glare of the Sun, and falls to a chilly –238 degrees F. at night. Such extremes are due partly to the slow rotation of the Moon, where a "day" is four of our weeks long. There is ample time for the surface to heat up by day, and equally long for it to cool off by night. If the Earth had no blanket of air, but still rotated once every twenty-

four hours, it might not have time to get quite so hot by
day or quite so cold by night. But the average temperature of such an airless Earth would be much the same
as the average temperature of the airless Moon—about
−13 degrees F (slightly more sophisticated calculations
suggest a temperature a few degrees warmer than this,
but still pretty cold). Since the present global mean air
temperature, in the layer of air just above the ground
or the surface of the sea, is about 59 degrees F, the
blanket of air must be contributing an overall warming
of about 72 degrees (a little less if the more sophisticated calculations are correct). Even if the Earth still
had an atmosphere, but it consisted only of nitrogen
and oxygen, which absorb very little infrared radiation,
the surface temperature would be almost as cold as −4
degrees F. The present comfortable warmth of the
globe is due to the powerful influence of relatively
small amounts of trace gases in the atmosphere, notably
carbon dioxide and water vapor. So, although human
activities have not as yet done much to change the
overall composition of the atmosphere, which is chiefly
nitrogen and oxygen, they have changed, significantly,
the balance of the trace gases that contribute most to
the greenhouse effect. There is no doubt that the Earth
will warm as a result, and some measurements suggest
that the warming has already begun. The important
questions are how quickly the world will warm, and
how the warming will change the patterns of wind and
weather worldwide.

Energy coming in from the Sun, remember, is
largely in the visible part of the spectrum and is not
absorbed in the atmosphere. Some ultraviolet radiation is absorbed in the stratosphere, and some incoming
solar energy is reflected away by clouds, or even by
the surface of the Earth (especially where deserts or
snowfields make the Earth's surface more reflective).
But the rest of the Sun's incoming energy goes to warm
the surface of the ground or of the sea. The warm

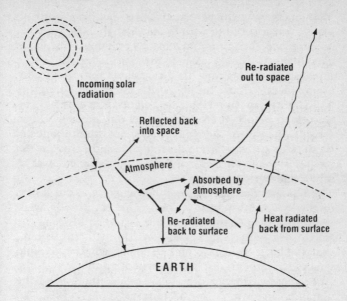

surface then radiates heat in the infrared part of the spectrum, mainly in the wavelength range from 4 to 100 micrometres.*

Some of this outgoing infrared radiation is absorbed strongly by water vapor and by carbon dioxide in the band from 13 to 100 micrometers. Water vapor also absorbs strongly between 4 and 7 micrometers, but between 7 and 13 micrometers there is a "window," where radiation used to escape fairly freely into space.

---

*A micrometer, one-millionth of a meter, is 1,000 times bigger than a nanometer (remember that a meter is 3.2 feet). When dealing with ultraviolet radiation, which has much shorter wavelengths than infrared radiation, nanometers (nm), were the appropriate units to use. When dealing with infrared, using nanometers would involve writing long strings of zeroes, so micrometers are preferred. If you want to compare these infrared figures with the ones for ultraviolet mentioned earlier, just multiply by 1,000 and you are back in nanometers.

Now, increasing quantities of CFCs, methane, and nitrous oxide associated with human activities are exerting an influence, beginning to close the window. But when climatologists first began to become alarmed at the prospect of an anthropogenic contribution to the greenhouse effect, adding to the natural effect and taking the temperature of the globe to heights not experienced since long before the emergence of our species, *Homo sapiens*, they were not concerned about the influence of these trace gases. Carbon dioxide was, and is, by far the biggest human contribution to the anthropogenic warming of the world.

The carbon dioxide greenhouse effect is not a new discovery. Atmospheric scientists in the 1860s were certainly aware of the role of trace gases in keeping the Earth pleasantly warm, and John Tyndall, in Britain, described the role of water vapor as what we would now call a "greenhouse gas" in a paper published in the *Philosophical Magazine* in 1863. Before the end of the nineteenth century, the Swede Svante Arrhenius had drawn attention, in a paper published in 1896, to the changes likely to be caused by the increasing amount of carbon dioxide getting into the air through combustion of coal, and the American P. C. Chamberlain wrote about the same problem in 1899. Throughout the first three-quarters of the present century, various climatologists had returned to the theme and made their own contributions to the debate about the greenhouse effect. It was generally agreed that the effect was real, and that it would make the Earth warmer. But it was only in 1975 that the prospect of a greenhouse warming of the globe gained widespread attention and became recognized as a problem that might have practical repercussions well within the lifetime of our present generation. This was also, of course, at about the time when people were beginning to appreciate the seriousness of the likely impact of CFCs on the ozone layer. To some extent, the timing is a coincidence, but it surely reflects also the growing awareness, among both scientists and the public at large, that in the last quarter of the twentieth century human influences on the environment could no longer be ignored.

THE CARBON DIOXIDE GREENHOUSE EFFECT

One reason why climatologists had become increasingly aware of the carbon dioxide problem during the 1960s was that in the preceding decade a monitoring station keeping tabs on the gas had been established on top of Mauna Loa, in Hawaii. That site was chosen for the carbon dioxide monitoring station because it was high on a mountain, in the middle of an ocean, where the measurements would be free from contamination by industrial pollution. For similar reasons, another monitoring station has been established at the South Pole. Both showed a steady buildup of the concentration of carbon dioxide in the atmosphere, confirming the fears based on calculations of how much coal and oil were being burned around the world. In 1957, the concentration of carbon dioxide in the atmosphere was about 315 parts per million (ppm). It is now above 345 ppm (or, if you prefer, 0.034 percent), and estimates based on the analysis of carbon from tree rings suggest that the baseline from which this growth took off in 1850, with the worldwide spread of the industrial revolution, was about 270 ppm.

The experts still argue about how much of the increase of carbon dioxide is due directly to burning coal and oil and how much might be blamed on deforestation. Cutting down trees on a large scale, as happened when the pioneers spread westward across North

America in the nineteenth century, and is happening today in the forests of South America, contributes directly to the carbon dioxide buildup when the trees are burned or decay; it also has an effect because there are fewer trees around to take carbon dioxide out of the air and use it for growth. The consensus today seems to be that the forest effect is more or less in balance, although it may have made a major contribution to the increase in carbon dioxide concentrations in the late nineteenth century. Since accurate monitoring of carbon dioxide began in the 1950s, therefore, roughly half of all the carbon dioxide produced by burning fuel has stayed in the atmosphere. The rest goes into various sinks, including some that is dissolved in the oceans, and some that may be taken up by plants that grow more efficiently when there is more carbon dioxide available. Whether these sinks will continue to operate in the same way in the future, as the carbon dioxide builds up further, nobody can say. The only reasonable guess is that roughly half of the carbon dioxide produced by human activities will continue to stay in the atmosphere. Since energy use is increasing worldwide, this means that the carbon dioxide concentration will not only continue to increase but will increase at a faster rate in the immediate future.

Assessments of how big an effect the buildup of carbon dioxide will have on temperature had varied widely in the 1960s (and before) depending on the assumptions used by the theorists in their calculations. In 1975, Stephen Schneider, of the National Center for Atmospheric Research, attempted to clear up the confusion by looking at the assumptions made by different groups of researchers and the ways they had worked their calculations through in their computer models. Because carbon dioxide is such a minor constituent of the atmosphere, none of these models could make any predictions of the changes that might result from any change in carbon dioxide short of doubling (or halving) the concentration. Even then, the estimates of the temperature increase due to a doubling of the concentration of carbon dioxide varied from a low of 1.3 degrees F to a high of 17.3 degrees F. When Schneider checked out each model in detail, comparing it both with other models and with the temperature patterns of the real world, he was able to narrow down the range, resolving the discrepancies and asserting with some confidence that doubling the carbon dioxide concentration would cause a rise in global mean temperatures of between 2.7 and 4.3 degrees F. In the same year, Syukuro Manabe and Richard Wetherald, of Princeton University, published the results of new calculations using what was at the time one of the most complete computer models of the atmosphere ever developed. They, too, came up with a warming of about 3.5 degrees F for a doubling of atmospheric carbon dioxide.

The consensus that, as a rule of thumb, doubling the carbon dioxide concentration from the background level of 270 ppm will increase global mean temperatures by 3.5 degrees F was established, and it has stood up throughout the past decade and a half, as improved computer models have refined the calculations. It was brought to the attention of a wide audience in 1975, as much by luck as judgment, in a paper in *Science* written by Wallace Broecker, of the Lamont-Doherty Geological Observatory.

Broecker had become interested in the greenhouse effect, and carried out some rule-of-thumb calculations, starting off from one of the older computer models that predicted a rise in temperatures of about 4 degrees F for a doubling of carbon dioxide. The choice of that particular model is where the luck comes in, though no doubt Broecker would prefer to say it showed his good judgment. By assuming that each 10 percent increase in carbon dioxide concentration would, therefore, cause an increase in global mean temperatures of half a degree F (an assumption which is simply that—a guess—since no computer model even today can tell us what effect such a small change in carbon dioxide will have), he came up with the prediction that the exponential growth in the amount of carbon dioxide in the atmosphere would take temperatures at the end of the twentieth century higher than they had been for at least the past thousand years. The carbon dioxide problem was out of the box, and has been subjected to increasing attention from climatologists ever since. Only now, they don't just have carbon dioxide to worry about.

OTHER GREENHOUSE GASES

The climate researcher who is generally credited with having blown the whistle on CFCs as greenhouse gases is Veerhabadrhan Ramanathan, who was working at the NASA-Langley Research Center in 1975 and is now at the University of Chicago. In a feature in *Time* magazine on October, 19, 1987, for example, Ramanathan is said to have been "amazed" to discover, in 1975, that CFCs are strong infrared absorbers. With his work as a basis, the National Academy of Sciences report on CFCs in 1976 included a mention of the greenhouse effect, and noted that if the rate at which CFCs were being released was held to 1973 levels, their contribution to global warming would be something less than half the increase due to the buildup of carbon dioxide by the year 2000. But if the release of CFCs grew at 10 percent a year, their influence would exceed that of the carbon dioxide produced by human activities before the end of the present century. In the longer term, said the report, increasing release of CFCs to the atmosphere, even at a growth of only a few percent a year, could lead to climatic changes of "drastic proportions."

Perhaps Ramanathan would have been slightly less amazed, however, if he had read the report of the International Conference on the Ecology and Toxicology of Fluorocarbons, a meeting held in Andover, Maine, in November 1973. There, Jim Lovelock had conceded that there was a conceivable way in which CFCs could become a danger to the global environment. He pointed out that if and when the concentration of CFCs in the atmosphere increased tenfold from the levels of the early 1970s, it would be a significant contributor to the greenhouse effect (it has now reached that concentration). He seems to have been the first scientist to identify CFCs as a potentially hazardous greenhouse gas, and he suggested that this might be a much more important problem than any damage that might be done to the ozone layer—and, in spite of recent events over Antarctica, he might well be correct.

At the end of the 1980s, the greenhouse effect already looks much more alarming than it did to Broecker in the middle of the 1970s. In the developed world, demand for energy has leveled off as population growth has decreased and people have achieved an affluent, energy-rich way of life. But in the Third World, economic growth is the only way people have of achieving the affluent "Western" lifestyle that is now regarded as so attractive, and economic growth means using an increasing amount of fuel, largely fossil fuel in the form of coal. The overall result is that global use of fossil fuel is increasing at a rate of about 4 percent a year, which implies a doubling in the amount of fuel burned each year after sixteen years have passed.

There are enormous quantities of coal available in the ground, so that this dramatic increase in energy use is certainly possible. At present rates of consumption, coal reserves would last for more than a thousand years; even with unrestricted growth in consumption (but assuming growth slows down as the Third World catches up with the rich), the amount burned each year would probably peak only in the twenty-second century, at five times the present rates, before beginning to decline as reserves ran out. (It is worth mentioning, perhaps, that even this frantic combustion of coal would pose no threat to the oxygen content of the atmosphere. There is so much oxygen in the air that even burning all the available fossil fuel into carbon dioxide would reduce the oxygen concentration by only 1 or 2 percent.) Carbon dioxide concentrations could easily reach a value double that of the preindustrial level by the year 2030, on this basis. But as we move into the 1990s, there is probably already as big a contribution to the anthropogenic greenhouse effect from other trace gases as the present excess of carbon dioxide above the preindustrial level. The implication is that marked changes in the climate are likely to happen before the year 2000.

Because carbon dioxide is still the biggest contributor to the anthropogenic greenhouse effect, and because it was the first to be identified, the experts measure the greenhouse effect of other trace gases in terms of their carbon dioxide equivalent—this also makes it easier to take on board and update the estimates of future climatic changes based on the carbon dioxide effect alone, simply by adding in the appropriate extra amount of carbon dioxide. The biggest single effect, after carbon dioxide, comes from methane, which is at present producing about 36 percent as much effect as the present excess of carbon dioxide. Ozone in the troposphere, CFCs other than F-11 and F-12, and extra water vapor resulting from the greenhouse warming of the oceans are lumped together for the purposes of these calculations, and are together estimated to be producing about 29 percent of the carbon dioxide effect. F-11 and F-12, taken together, contribute a further 29 percent, and nitrous oxide about 9 percent. Adding these figures together, the extra warming of the globe due to these trace gases is already likely to be about 3 percent more than the increase in temperatures caused by the increase in concentrations of carbon dioxide from 270 ppm to above 340 ppm. In that same *Time* article, Stephen Schneider was quoted as providing an apt summing-up of the situation: "These are the little guys," he said, "but they nickel and dime you to the point where they add up to 50 percent of the problem." And James Hansen, of the Nasa-Goddard Institute for Space Studies, has estimated, on the basis of a Goddard climate model that takes more account of the trace gases than most such computer simulations do, that the global warming will reach a couple degrees F above preindustrial levels within the next twenty years, taking it not just to temperatures higher than any experienced, as a global mean, for a thousand years, but higher than anything experienced for a *hundred* thousand years. "Ten years from now," Hansen is quoted as saying in a special issue of *Chemical & Engineering News* (November 24, 1986) devoted to the changing atmosphere, "everyone will start asking what can be done." Why are they likely to be worried? What exactly would a seemingly modest increase of a degree or so in global temperatures mean for the world's climate?

THE LONG-TERM PERSPECTIVE

One way to get a grasp of how dramatic a change this will be is by looking back over the past to see how long it is since the world experienced conditions as warm as we are likely to see in the twenty-first century. The conditions that have existed on Earth for the past few million years (roughly speaking, over the entire span of the evolution of the *Homo* line) are not "normal" in a longer-term perspective of hundreds of millions of years. Throughout most of its history, geological evidence shows, the Earth has not had even one permanent ice cap throughout the year, let alone two. Ice caps usually form only when there is land near to one or other of the poles, where snow can settle and build up into ice sheets. The frozen Arctic sea today is a special case, surrounded by land and kept cold enough for ice to form because warm water from the tropics cannot penetrate into the polar ocean. As the continents drift slowly about the globe, colliding and breaking up into new geographical patterns, it just happens that every couple of hundred million years or so conditions are right for an ice cap to form, and then the world enters an ice epoch. Within an ice epoch, there may be intervals of particularly severe cold, ice ages proper, or temporary respites in which the ice retreats back into its polar fastness. Such a little warm interval is called an interglacial, and we live in an interglacial that began, roughly speaking, 10,000 years ago.

It is impossible to set accurate figures on the temperatures that prevailed before the present ice epoch began, but the Arctic ice sheet has existed for well over 2 million years, and during all that time global mean temperature can never have been more than 4.5 degrees F higher than today, according to a study carried out by Herman Flohn for the International Institute for Applied Systems Analysis, in Austria. In broad outline, the geological records indicate that the period from about 100 million years ago to 65 million years ago (the last part of the Mesozoic Era) was substantially warmer than today. Dinosaurs and "tropical" vegetation flourished even at high latitudes, including those of Canada and Siberia. By about 55 million years ago, the climate was in decline as the world cooled, probably as a result of geographical changes associated with continental drift. Antarctic ice was growing by 10 million years ago, and by 4 million years ago it had reached its present extent. By some definitions, that provides the starting date for the present ice epoch, although continental ice sheets first appeared in the Northern Hemisphere only about 3 million years ago.

During the ice epoch, shifts from full ice age to interglacial conditions are associated with changes in global mean temperature of only about 9 degrees F—that is, the temperatures during the ice age that ended about 10,000 years ago were only 9 degrees F cooler, on average, than the temperature of the globe today. The warmest interglacial of the entire period of the current ice epoch—certainly the warmest interval for at least the past 2 million years—occurred during the interglacial previous to our own, something over 120,000 years ago, when temperatures peaked at an average some 4.5 degrees F higher than global mean temperatures today. At that time, hippopotamuses, lions, and forest elephants roamed southern England. But throughout the past 2 million years or more, interglacials have been rare, periods roughly 10,000 years long sandwiched between the full ice ages, themselves roughly 100,000 years long. By the time the anthropogenic greenhouse effect has warmed the world by about 5.5 degrees F, which seems likely to happen sometime in the twenty-first century, the world will be warmer than it has been at any time during the past 2 or 3 million years, and well on the way back toward the conditions that the dinosaurs enjoyed so much.

In some ways, such a warmer world might seem a more comfortable place for life—certainly preferable to a return of full ice age conditions. But the transition from the world to which we are accustomed to a warmer world could be painful, especially when the ice caps start to melt.

LIVING IN A WARMER WORLD

Although we are all used to temperature changes of a couple of degrees, or more, that is quite different from the implications of an overall rise of 1 or 2 degrees in world temperatures. First, computer calculations and comparisons of warm and cold years in the real world show that when the world warms, the high latitudes warm most and the region around the equator warms least. So an increase of 2 degrees F in global mean temperatures may mean a much bigger increase near the poles, at the latitudes of the northern United States and Europe, for example. Secondly, temperature changes also imply changes in rainfall and in wind patterns. Some regions of the world will get wetter, and some drier, when the world warms; reliable winds that bring monsoon rains may change their tracks; and, according to some studies, storms may become more common. Several studies also suggest that, paradoxically, severe winters may be more common in some regions as the world warms—a modest rise in average temperatures over the whole year may, in some places, conceal a bigger rise in temperatures in summer, and the possibility of a drop in winter temperatures.

The computer models cannot deal satisfactorily with such subtleties. The computers make their calculations on the basis of a grid of positions covering the globe, where one point in the grid may represent the average conditions of a region as large as one of the states of the United States or of a European country. In the computer, properties such as temperature and cloud cover are defined only by the grid points. So, for example, as far as the computer is concerned, the temperature over all of Colorado is the same, while the cloud cover over Britain consists either of a uniform bank of cloud or of no cloud at all (some of the models do not even acknowledge the existence of such details as the British Isles). There is also the problem of the oceans. Some 70 percent of the surface of the globe is covered by water, and the oceans store up heat—they "remember" past conditions, so that they both warm up and cool down more slowly than do the continents. That is why the climate of Britain, an island nestling at the edge of an ocean, is so different from the climate of continental Europe. But no computer model yet devised deals with the oceans in a fully satisfactory way. Although the computer models are useful at giving the broad outline, details of how the real world is likely to respond to the warming of the greenhouse effect are better indicated, at present, by looking at how warm and cold years in the real world have compared in the past.

This approach has been applied with great success by a team at the University of East Anglia, in Britain. Accurate records of temperature and rainfall over most of the land area of the Northern Hemisphere go back only to 1925, so initially the team concentrated on the period since then, picking out the five warmest and five coldest years from the records and combining the data from the years at each extreme to produce composite "warm Earth" and "cold Earth" scenarios. For the fifty

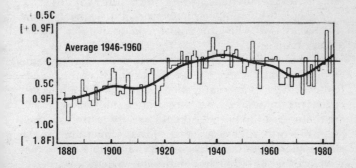

years from 1925 to 1974, the five coldest years were 1964, 1965, 1966, 1968, and 1972. The five warmest years were 1937, 1938, 1943, 1944, and 1953. When each set of five years is averaged, and then the two composite "years" are compared with one another region by region, they show just the kind of variations of temperature change with latitude that the computer models suggest, but give more detail of regional changes. The overall temperature difference between the warm and cold composites is about 1 degree F, but the region above 65° N was 3 degrees F warmer in the warm set of years than in the cold composite. The tropics show barely any temperature change.

Looking around the world, the comparison shows that a region from Finland across the Soviet Union eastward to 90° E warms by more than 5.5 degrees F, while the United States warms by only 2 to 4 degrees F, and some parts of the world, including Japan, India, Turkey, and Spain, show a small decrease in temperature. Hand in hand with these changes, although the warm composite shows almost 2 percent more rainfall over land than in the cold composite (exactly what you would expect, if more water evaporates from the seas in a warmer world), the change is very unevenly distributed. India and the Middle East experience a bigger than average increase, while the United States, Europe, and the grain-growing region of the Soviet Union all suffer a decline in rainfall, along with a rise in temperature.

This could be a recipe for disaster, if the same pattern holds when the greenhouse effect begins to exert its grip. A combination of higher temperatures and less rainfall is the prescription for drought and perhaps dustbowl conditions, especially in regions such as the North American great plains, which are on the knife edge of desertification today. It seems likely that the continuing droughts in the sub-Saharan region of Africa (the Sahel) and across eastward into Ethiopia may be related to precisely this kind of change, caused by the developing greenhouse effect.

Following their success with this method of modeling the links between overall temperature changes and regional rainfall and temperature patterns, the University of East Anglia team decided to see what they could deduce by comparing a genuinely warm *run* of years with a comparable succession of cold years. In Europe and North America, at least, they were able to find sufficiently accurate records going back to the beginning of the present century. These show that the coldest set of twenty consecutive years was from 1901 to 1920, while the warmest sequence of twenty consecutive years was from 1934 to 1953. In this geographically more limited, but scientifically more securely based, study they found that even though spring, summer, and autumn are all warmer in Europe in the warm decades, there was a greater occurrence of cold winters over the whole of central Europe, in a band of latitudes covering 10° either side of latitude 50° N. They could also identify the reasons for the change, which have to do with changes in atmospheric circulation that make persistent high-pressure systems, known as "blocking highs," more common. These blocking highs stop warm westerlies from the Atlantic penetrating into mainland Europe.

The conclusions of the University of East Anglia team, including the prediction that a greenhouse warming would bring more severe winters in Europe, was published in 1984. Britain and other parts of Europe were promptly struck by three vicious winters in a row, in 1984–85, 1985–86, and 1986–87. The cause? Persistent, "unseasonable" blocking high systems that became established over northwestern Europe.

Taking the whole period since 1850, and making the best assessment of the limited temperature records that are available in the years before 1925, the team concludes that average global air temperatures have risen by about 1 degree F. This slow rise in average

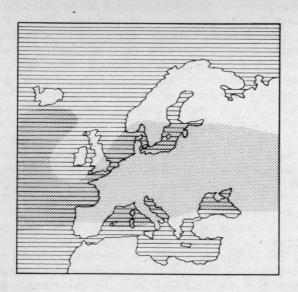

temperatures is nowhere near as big as the erratic fluctuations from year to year and decade to decade, but it is almost exactly in line with calculations based on the growing carbon dioxide greenhouse effect. Other factors that may be at work, producing some of those fluctuations, include volcanic eruptions, which throw dust into the stratosphere, where it can stay for months or years and act as a temporary sunshield that allows the Earth below to cool, and variations in the Sun itself. But by 1987 the "signal" of the greenhouse warming seemed to be established. Five of the nine warmest years on record, up to 1987, had occurred since 1978, and 1980, 1981, and 1983 stand out from the record as the three warmest years since record-keeping began.

So the greenhouse effect is being taken more seriously now than ever before, and the possibility that gases such as CFCs may combine to double the anthropogenic carbon dioxide effect only adds urgency to the growing debate. One problem that has been highlighted recently is the rise in sea levels, which has been going on throughout the twentieth century and seems likely to continue at an increasing rate in the decades ahead. Part of this increase is caused by water being added to the oceans as glaciers and ice caps melt slightly in a warmer world; part is caused simply by the thermal expansion of the surface layers of water as the oceans begin to warm. Between 1880 and 1985, sea levels rose by between 4 and 6 inches. By the end of the twenty-first century, with global mean temperatures perhaps 9 degrees F higher than today, the rise in sea levels could reach a yard or so. Hardly surprisingly, low-lying Holland is now taking a lead in trying to persuade the European community to take action in investigating the greenhouse effect and seeking ways to minimize its impact.

Predictions so far, of course, have been based on the assumption that atmospheric conditions will change smoothly as the greenhouse effect gathers strength. As I have already mentioned, the most disturbing aspect of the discovery of a hole in the ozone layer over Antarctica is the message this carries that the atmosphere does in fact respond in *non*linear fashion, at least to some disturbances. There is now immense pressure on the climatologists to try to provide at least some warning of similar dramatic changes in regional climates that may result when the concentration of carbon dioxide and other greenhouse gases in the atmosphere reaches some critical level. All that, however, is outside the scope of this book. What is relevant, and very much so, is the importance of the greenhouse effect for conditions in the stratosphere.

INFLUENCES ON OZONE

The stratosphere is warmer than the troposphere because ozone in the stratosphere absorbs incoming ultraviolet radiation from the Sun (ozone is unusual in its
contribution to the heat balance of the Earth; unlike
other trace gases, it absorbs *both* infrared and ultraviolet radiation). As we saw in chapter 4, although interactions involving CFCs and other compounds at high
altitudes are destroying ozone at around 25 miles above
the ground, other interactions, involving methane in
particular, are producing an increase in the amount of
ozone present at lower altitudes in some parts of the
world. This increase is also caused partly by a process
known as "self-healing." When the ozone high in the
stratosphere is depleted, more solar ultraviolet can
penetrate to lower altitudes, where it may interact
with oxygen to produce ozone. The self-healing effect is
strongest over the equator, where sunlight is strongest.
In terms of providing protection for ground-based life
from the harmful effects of the ultraviolet itself, this
effect is reassuring—in line with the name—although it
is rather small at the higher latitudes, where there is
most cause for concern about increased risk of skin
cancer. But in terms of the climatic changes that are
now going on in the atmosphere, associated with the
greenhouse effect, this redistribution of ozone may be
as alarming as a straightforward reduction in its concentration throughout the stratosphere.

Sherry Rowland put some numbers into these calculations in a lecture he gave at the University of North
Carolina at Chapel Hill, on March 11, 1987; the lecture
has been published in the "Carolina Environmental
Essay Series." As Rowland put it in that talk, "The
greenhouse warming and stratospheric ozone depletion
will occur in the same atmosphere, and their effects not

only will be intertwined, but also will perturb one another." Using an estimate that the temperature increase due to the greenhouse effect will be about 5.5 degrees F in terms of global mean sea level temperatures by the middle of the twenty-first century, Rowland infers a fall in temperatures of the high stratosphere of 18 degrees F. But this is not the only effect at work.

"The most important direct stratospheric physical effect from the depletion of ozone," says Rowland, "will be the reduced input there of incoming ultraviolet radiation." This is the energy input that makes the region of the stratosphere between 25 and 30 miles altitude hotter than the regions of the atmosphere immediately above and immediately below, and the absorption of UV by ozone is responsible for the existence of the stratosphere as a distinct layer of the atmosphere. Any change in energy absorption at these altitudes has an immediate effect on the temperature structure of the atmosphere, and in the long term—on the same time scale as the greenhouse effect perturbation used in Rowland's calculations—the continuing release of CFCs at present rates will cause a depletion of at least 50 percent in the ozone content around 25 miles altitude. This will lead to a decrease in temperature of this crucial region of the atmosphere of about 36 degrees F. The combined effect of ozone depletion and the greenhouse effect will, therefore, cause a total temperature drop in the upper stratosphere of 54 degrees F, which Rowland describes as "a very substantial alteration."

At the same time, of course, the lower layers of the atmosphere will be warming as a result of the greenhouse effect and, at some altitudes and some latitudes, because of the self-healing process. It is quite impossible, at present, to calculate what effects these changes will have on world weather patterns, but throwing such a large wrench into the works of the weather machine must surely have some influence on its workings.

The one potential silver lining in all of this was the

suggestion that by making the stratosphere cooler, the greenhouse effect would slow down the rates of the chemical reactions that are scavenging ozone. That may be true over a large part of the globe. But one of the key facts that emerged from the Dahlem meeting in November 1987 was that very cold conditions in the stratosphere over Antarctica are implicated in the particular chemical processes that are now thought to be responsible for the sudden development of the ozone hole each spring. Although temperature changes due to ozone depletion and the greenhouse effect are as yet nowhere near as big as the ones Rowland projects for the middle of the next century, it is quite possible that the greenhouse effect may already have played a part in tipping the balance of conditions in the atmosphere over Antarctica into a state that favors the growth of the hole in the sky.

CHAPTER SIX

THE HOLE OVER ANTARCTICA

The hole in the sky was first noticed by a team of researchers from the British Antarctic Survey, working at Halley Bay, in Antarctica, in 1982. Regular observations have been made at the same site, throughout the months from October to March, every year since 1957, the International Geophysical Year. At that time, a coordinated international scientific effort was made to investigate our planetary environment. It was so successful that the "year" actually ran for two years, and among the spinoffs from it were the launching of the space satellite programs of both the United States and the Soviet Union, and continuing scientific studies of Antarctica, and the atmosphere above the southernmost continent, by teams from several nations. In light of the discoveries now being made, with instruments on the ground, in the air, and from satellites, it seems that a similar major international scientific effort is needed to determine just what is going on in the stratosphere at present.

When Joe Farman and his colleagues first noticed strange depletions of ozone in the air above the Antarctic, they were using an old instrument that had been in service for some time. This kind of instrument, a spectrophotometer, measures the concentration of ozone in a column of the atmosphere by taking the spectroscopic fingerprint of ozone. All molecules in the air absorb precisely defined, characteristic wavelengths of light (different for each molecule) as sunlight passes through the atmosphere. By recording the strength of the characteristic lines associated with, in this case, ozone molecules, in the spectrum of visible light, the instrument determines how much ozone there is between the spectrophotometer, on the ground, and the top of the atmosphere. Since it needs sunlight in order to measure the spectrum, this particular type of instrument cannot tell us anything about ozone concentrations during the long polar winter night. But what it began to tell the Halley Bay team about springtime ozone concentrations (those in September and October, in the Southern Hemisphere) was sufficiently startling for them to stand back and take a cautious second look before making any sensational announcements in the scientific press.

THE HOLE APPEARS

Farman and his colleagues had no reason to suspect that their old instrument had suddenly gone haywire, but they had a new instrument, calibrated carefully back in England, just becoming available, and they thought it best to wait and double-check their observations with the new spectrophotometer. Besides, they knew that American researchers had two experiments that were monitoring the ozone content of the stratosphere from the weather satellite *Nimbus 7*. The satellite had been in orbit since 1978, and those instruments (the Total Ozone Mapping Spectrometer, or TOMS; and the Solar Backscatter Ultraviolet, or SBUV, experiment) should have easily detected the kind of dramatic drop in springtime ozone concentrations that they were measuring from Halley Bay. But none of the published satellite data gave any hint of a springtime "hole" in the ozone layer over Antarctica, even though the 1982 Halley Bay observations suggested that more than 20 percent of the ozone overhead disappeared during October. Caution seemed to be in order.

By October 1984, however, the British Antarctic Survey team was sure. The new instrument confirmed the trend, and reported that in October 1984 the depletion of ozone over Halley Bay amounted to more than 30 percent. At the same time, measurements from another ground station, a thousand miles to the north, confirmed a loss of ozone from the stratosphere. It wasn't just a local effect happening over the Halley Bay site. The observations in 1983 and 1984 were particularly significant also because there is a certain amount of uncertainty in all measurements of this kind—scientists seldom plot such observational points on a graph, as in figure 10 (see p. 114), without including "error bars" that indicate the range of uncertainties in the measurements. The 1982 measurements were low, but not so dramatically far below the bottom limits on the error bars of earlier measurements; the 1983 and 1984 measurements were so low that they simply could not be the result of errors in the measurements.

The trend has continued. In 1985, the concentration was lower still, and although the ozone concentrations measured by this and other techniques were not quite as low in the spring of 1986 as in the spring of 1985, by October 1987 they had reached the lowest values ever recorded over Antarctica, with more than 50 percent of the ozone in the stratosphere being destroyed in the spring, before a recovery—or, at least, a partial recovery—set in with the arrival of Antarctic summer. The percentages can be put in perspective by looking at the units these instruments actually measure in, called Dobson units, after the pioneering Oxford professor who developed the spectroscopic technique for measuring stratospheric ozone. One way of interpreting these measurements is to express them in terms of the thickness the ozone layer would have if all the ozone overhead were brought down to sea level pressure and a standard temperature of 32 degrees F. One Dobson unit is then equivalent to one thousandth of a centimeter of ozone. Between 1957 and the middle of the 1970s, the concentration of ozone over Halley Bay in October, coming out of Antarctic winter, was always about 300 Dobson units, corresponding to a thickness of about a tenth of an inch at standard temperature and pressure. In October 1987, the comparable figure was 125 Dobson units, corresponding to a sea level thickness of just .05 inches. This is what the researchers mean when they say that half the ozone layer has been destroyed (but remember that the ozone layer over Antarctica does recover in summer, even if not quite to the levels of the 1970s).

So why, then, had the *Nimbus 7* instruments failed to detect the change in the stratosphere in the early 1980s? When Farman and his colleagues published the scientific paper announcing the discovery of what became known as the ozone hole (the paper arrived at the *Nature* office on Christmas Eve, 1984, and appeared in print in the May 16, 1985, issue of the journal), they caused a flurry of activity at the Goddard Space Flight Center, responsible for the TOMS and SBUV experiments. The reason why the Goddard team failed to find the hole first soon became clear. Richard Stolarski, of NASA, recalls how the team had placed too much faith in the historical records of ozone measurements, and too little in their own instruments. At the time the satellite was launched, late in 1978, nobody had ever measured stratospheric ozone concentrations lower than a range "in the 200s" in Dobson units, he told me. Data coming back to Goddard from the satellite were processed automatically by computers before ever being touched by human hand (or seen by human eye), and the computers that processed the data had been programmed to reject any measurement lower than 180 Dobson units, and treat it as an anomaly. In their processing, the programs flagged the measurement as an anomaly, and reset it to 180 Dobson units for the purposes of their calculations—but, fortunately as it turns out, they also saved the original "erroneous" measurement without processing it further. The idea was that any such low readings would be subjected to further investigation at a later date, but somehow the researchers hadn't got around to this by the time the news from Halley Bay broke. One reason for this, says Stolarski, was that observations from the South Pole, by other American researchers, had not shown such low ozone concentrations in the early 1980s; there was a disagreement between the South Pole data and the satellite, and on later inspection it turned out that the error was at the pole. At the time, however, this discrepancy reinforced the assumption by the Goddard team that satellite measurements below about 200 Dobson units could be ignored. Even though very low values, 180 Dobson units, could show up in the processed data, they were flagged as erroneous, so none of the researchers took much notice of them.

The story is important, not just because of the amusement afforded to outsiders by seeing the Goddard scientists shoot themselves in the foot. It would have been just as easy for them to have programmed their computers so that measurements of ozone concentrations below 180 Dobson units rang bells, flashed lights and alerted them to something remarkable. The point is that in the late 1970s and early 1980s atmospheric scientists were increasingly confident that they understood, more or less, what was going on in the atmosphere. Both the chemistry and the dynamics of air movements were being analyzed in more detail than ever before, and a coherent picture was emerging. But nowhere in that coherent picture was there even a hint that a dramatic change like the development of a huge hole in the ozone layer could occur. The lesson afforded by the shock of this discovery ought to echo throughout the whole of science—*always* expect the unexpected; *never* trust your models implicitly.

When the import of the British observations hit them, the NASA scientists were able to go back to the original data and instruct the computers to take them at face value. When they did so, both the ozone monitoring instruments showed not only that the springtime ozone hole existed, but also that it extended over the entire Antarctic continent. It soon became clear that the depletion was mainly concentrated in a layer of the atmosphere between about 6 and 15 miles altitude, with some lesser depletion of ozone around 25 miles. The "hole in the sky" is actually more like a slice out of the atmosphere, a pancake covering Antarctica—a "hole" as deep as Mount Everest is tall, and covering an area as big as the continental United States. It shows up in the computer processed images (correctly computer processed, now!) from the TOMS data, one of which is shown on the cover of this book.

CHEMICAL CONNECTIONS

That *Nature* paper also set the cat among the chemical pigeons. Since the early 1970s, the researchers at Halley Bay had also been monitoring the concentrations of

CFCs in the atmosphere. These had been increasing markedly, and it was natural for the team to wonder if there was any connection between the increase in CFC concentrations and the decrease in springtime ozone concentrations. The graph of ozone depletion they published in *Nature* had, superimposed on it, the trend of F-11 and F-12 concentrations measured at the same site, plotted in such a way that concentration is *greater* at the bottom of the graph (essentially the same as figure 10). The two curves matched closely—or, if the concentration of CFCs is plotted in the conventional way, increasing up the page, the two curves mirror each other. This didn't prove that there was a cause and effect relationship, but as the team pointed out in that paper, "the present-day atmosphere differs most prominently from that of previous decades in the higher concentrations of halocarbons." They suggested that the very low temperatures over Antarctica from midwinter to early spring might make the stratosphere there "uniquely sensitive to the growth of inorganic chlorine," an assessment that has now been born out by two and a half years of intensive research. The reasons for all that frantic activity were put in a nutshell by Farman in an article in *New Scientist* on November 12, 1987. "Prior to 1985," he said, "atmospheric chemists all thought that they were getting somewhere with their understanding of ozone. Observations and models agreed. Observed and predicted changes were less than 1 percent per decade. However, over Antarctica the depletion is now more than 50 percent, and this over a period of between 30 and 40 days each year."

The theorists had first crack at the problem, since by May 1985 it was too late to set up any major scientific expeditions to Antarctica for the coming southern spring. Three main lines of attack were pursued in the rest of 1985 and into 1986. Some researchers concentrated on the chemistry of the stratosphere over Antarctica, trying

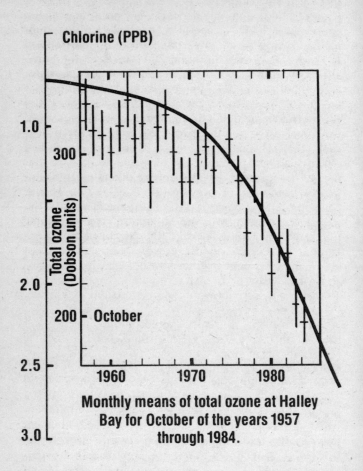

Monthly means of total ozone at Halley Bay for October of the years 1957 through 1984.

to find ways in which the unusually cold wintertime conditions there might set things up so that when the Sun returned in the spring it would trigger a burst of photochemical activity which drained ozone out of the stratosphere. Others suggested that the problem might not be one of ozone *depletion*, but of *redistribution*, with air originating from higher latitudes and lower altitudes, poor in ozone, pushing into the Antarctic in springtime and rising up into the stratosphere, displacing the ozone layer. All such "dynamic" theories tied the changes in Antarctic ozone to changes in the atmospheric circulation around the southern hemisphere over the same period of time. And a minority view linked the changes in Antarctic ozone with the changing activity of the Sun, which had reached a peak in 1979 and had been declining during the period of dramatic growth in the ozone hole. This is, essentially, a small-scale version (complicated by the need to build in a delay between peak solar activity and maximum ozone depletion) of the "death of the dinosaurs" scenario suggested by Crutzen and his colleagues; a key feature of this is that it implicates NO_x in the ozone destruction process.

Among the many scientific papers published touching on these topics in 1985 and 1986, several are worth picking out, with the benefit of hindsight. As plans were laid in the United States for a National Ozone Expedition (NOZE) to travel to McMurdo Station in Antarctica for observations in the southern spring of 1986, the journal *Geophysical Research Letters* invited scientists to contribute papers to a special supplement which would sum up the state of theoretical ideas on the subject, and observations to date, as a background to that mission. The supplement appeared in November 1986, and includes some ideas which were being proved wrong even as the journal went to press, but others which have stood the test of time. In their contribution to the supplement, Patrick Hamill, Brian Toon and Richard Turco, three researchers based in California, were among several teams to draw attention in 1986 to a possible link between high altitude clouds over Antarctica and the formation of the ozone hole. These clouds, called Polar Stratospheric Clouds, or PSCs, form a tenuous haze in the lower stratosphere over Antarctica in the winter months. The clouds dissipate in the spring, exactly at the same time and in the same place that the hole is forming. The California-based team proposed that a series of chemical reactions taking place on the surfaces of particles in these clouds during the winter months might be locking up water and nitrogen compounds, and releasing chlorine in an active form that could react with ozone as the sunlight returned.

Earlier in the year, two other teams had put forward their own chemical ideas in *Nature*, both invoking PSCs but favoring different detailed chemical models. Mike McElroy and his colleagues came up with a suggestion that bromine compounds might be involved; Susan Solomon, of the National Oceanographic and Atmospheric Administration, and several colleagues, including Sherry Rowland, concentrated on reactions involving chlorine and nitrogen compounds. And in the last issue of *Nature* for 1986, Paul Crutzen and Frank Arnold, now working in Germany, independently came up with yet another similar suggestion, invoking a slightly different set of chemical reactions but also implicating PSCs in the processes that "preconditioned" the Antarctic stratosphere in winter and set up the possibility of ozone depletion in spring. "In the Antarctic lower stratosphere during winter and springtime," they concluded, "unstable photochemical conditions can develop that lead to drastic destruction of ozone."

All of this activity among the theorists depended on two things—the presence of PSCs, and the extreme cold of the Antarctic stratosphere. Or rather, it depended on the extreme cold, since the PSCs themselves form only when the stratosphere is cold enough.

In their contribution to the *Geophysical Research Letters* supplement, Paul Newman, of the Applied Research Corporation, in Landover, Maryland, and Mark Schoeberl, of NASA-Goddard, reported that October measurements of the temperature of air over Antarctica, obtained from instruments carried by unmanned balloons and satellites, showed a cooling in the lower stratosphere of 32.5 degrees F at about 15 miles altitude between October 1979 and October 1985. At the end of 1986, a link between extreme cold, the formation of PSCs, chemical reactions on the surfaces of cloud particles, and, ultimately, destruction of ozone was beginning to emerge as front-runner in the race to explain the ozone hole.

All of this had resulted from a few months' intensive work by the chemists—and I have by no means mentioned all of their activity during that time. Many of the names are familiar from the ozone debate of the 1970s; experienced scientists, deeply concerned about the possible harmful effects of CFCs. They had nothing new to go on, except the observation that an Antarctic hole existed, and they could have made the same calculations before—certainly months before, if not years before. But it took the observations to shake them out of the complacency alluded to by Farman in his *New Scientist* article, and typified by the assumption of the Goddard researchers that measurements of ozone concentrations below 180 Dobson units must be mistakes, and to start them thinking along new lines. In spite of their rapid advance toward a new understanding of the ozone layer over Antarctica (once they had been pointed in the right direction by the observations), at the end of 1986 rival theories were still in the running. When the data from National Ozone Experiment were fully assimilated, however, there seemed little doubt that chemistry was, indeed, the culprit.

A PROCESS OF ELIMINATION

Scientists who traveled to McMurdo Station in August 1986, for the National Ozone Experiment observed the stratosphere with the aid of instruments on the ground, looking upward, and packages carried on balloons. They also, of course, had the continuing observations from TOMS and SBUV, on *Nimbus 7*, to tie in to their own measurements. The observations they made would test the three main types of theory (with variations on each theme to complicate the issue), and they soon began to clear away some of the confusion of possible explanations that had sprung up since the British Antarctic Survey team had announced the existence of the hole. The first candidate to fall by the wayside was the model linking Antarctic ozone depletion with solar activity. Instead of finding increased concentrations of NO_x in the ozone depleted region, NOZE measured very low quantities—the lowest atmospheric nitrogen dioxide concentrations, in particular, ever measured anywhere in the world. Observations from New Zealand confirmed the trend; NO_2 was in short supply in the far Southern Hemisphere just when ozone was being destroyed. Theorists who favored the solar model, notably Linwood Callis, of the NASA-Langley Research Center, tried to gain some comfort from the fact that the ozone hole in 1986 was slightly less pronounced than in 1985. Perhaps 1985 had marked the low point of a cycle associated with solar activity, and the ozone was recovering precisely because the NO_x concentrations were low. But their remaining slender hopes were dashed when the 1987 hole turned out to be the deepest yet, and there was still no sign of the required nitrogen compounds. Besides, as many people had pointed out, there had been no trace of a similar ozone hole following either the solar maximum of the late 1950s or the one of the late 1960s.

Dynamical theories were harder to kill off. NOZE found no evidence of the rising air needed, according to this model, to displace ozone. But, after all, the observations were made from only one site, on the edge of the Antarctic continent. It took the bigger expedition of 1987 to really put the lid on this model, with the discovery that, if anything, air in the region of ozone depletion was descending from the very high atmosphere (incidentally, this means that the photochemical ozone destruction process, whatever it is, must be even *more* efficient than was originally suspected, since this falling air is bringing fresh ozone into the region where it is being destroyed). The idea that atmospheric dynamics might be the dominant force in causing the ozone depletion was certainly in retreat after NOZE; but a suspicion began to grow that dynamics might be implicated—*must* be implicated—in establishing the right conditions for the unusual chemical reactions that people such as McElroy, Susan Solomon, Crutzen, and many others saw as the immediate cause of ozone destruction.

Jerry Mahlman, of Princeton University, is especially interested in the link between changes in the circulation of the atmosphere and the cooling over Antarctica. He works with computer simulations of the atmosphere, models that show how the wind patterns change under different conditions. Under "normal" conditions, the conditions that prevailed in the Southern Hemisphere before about 1979, atmospheric waves from the troposphere at lower latitudes rise and move southward to lick down again toward the polar region. The downward motion both warms the air (falling air gets hot as the pressure builds up, just as the air in a bicycle pump gets hot when you pump it) and carries in ozone to the lower stratosphere. But Mahlman has found that, according to the computer model, this normal pattern is only barely stable. The model easily switches over into another stable state, where the tongues of air no longer lick so vigorously southward. If this happens in the real world and these waves are weaker, the winds blow in a more closely circular pattern around Antarctica, and the warming effect diminishes. There would also be less ozone around in the Antarctic stratosphere. The direct influence on ozone is too small to account for the hole, it is now recognized. But the change in circulation patterns, strengthening the circulation around Antarctica and producing a strong circumpolar vortex while allowing the stratosphere over the continent to cool more in winter than it did in the 1970s, may be an essential ingredient in the growth of the hole. Changes in atmospheric dynamics may establish a wintertime pattern of still, cold air over Antarctica, so cut off from the outside world that it might as well be sealed behind the walls of a chemist's reaction flask.

National Oceanographic and Atmospheric Administration researchers have shown that the kind of wave activity Mahlman describes *has* decreased in the 1980s—but nobody knows why.

While other theories were being eliminated, some NOZE observations provided direct evidence that ozone-destroying chemistry was at work. Balloons launched from McMurdo showed that the ozone depletion was confined to a band of the stratosphere between about 7.5 and 12.5 miles altitude, and that within that band the overall depletion was about 35 percent. But between 8 and 11.5 miles, the stratosphere lost more than 70 percent of its ozone, compared with the highest values observed in August, and on one occasion in October 1986 the observers noted that 90 percent of the ozone had disappeared from a layer of about 1 to 3 miles thick—the heart ripped out of the ozone layer. There were actually increases in the amount of ozone around 15 to 18 miles, associated with atmospheric wave activity, so total column measurements from the ground underestimated the severity of the depletion at lower altitudes. Other measurements on the same balloon flight that showed the most dramatic reductions in ozone concentrations showed no evidence of the kind of other changes, for example, in the aerosol particles, that would be expected if air depleted in ozone and other substances was somehow squeezing into the region from outside—the kind of particles found in the depleted layer were just like those in the layers above and below. It is hard for chemistry to explain the dramatic, small-scale variations—but it is impossible to explain them by dynamics.

Other observations pointed the finger firmly at chlorine compounds. Susan Solomon's team measured high concentrations of a form of chlorine dioxide, OClO (in which the chlorine atom sits between two oxygen atoms) in the hole. There was twenty to fifty times more chlorine dioxide than expected, and this particular form of chlorine dioxide (it also comes in a molecule with the chlorine atom on one end, ClOO) had never before been detected in the atmosphere, anywhere in the world. This was not the only oxide of chlorine present in surprising quantities; Philip Solomon and colleagues from the State University of New York (SUNY) used a beautiful technique borrowed from radio astronomy to measure high concentrations of chlorine monoxide, ClO, in the ozone hole.

The kind of spectrophotometer used by Farman and his colleagues to monitor ozone in the stratosphere depends on the tendency of the molecules to block out certain wavelengths of light from the Sun, passing through the atmosphere. Similar techniques are even sensitive enough to be used with moonlight. But the SUNY researchers measured, instead, the radiation actually produced by rotating molecules of chlorine monoxide in the air above them. These emissions occur in the microwave band, at a wavelength of just over 1 millimeter (.04 inches) for the ClO molecules. Both microwave emission and microwave absorption (the radio equivalent of the standard ozone spectroscopy technique) are used by radio astronomers to identify the chemical constituents of clouds in space millions of light-years from Earth. Measuring ClO in the stratosphere might seem easy by comparison but is complicated by the radio noise produced by other influences. Still, it can be done. The exact nature of the microwave signal depends on the pressure in the region where the molecules are located, so the technique not only reveals the presence of ClO, it tells the researchers at what altitude it is concentrated. Finally, the strength of the signal reveals how much ClO is there. Solomon and his colleagues found high concentrations of chlorine monoxide in the lower stratosphere, around 12.5 miles, where most of the ozone loss was occurring. The abundances were highest in early to mid-September, reaching concentrations between 0.5 and 2 parts per billion (ppb), when the ozone was rapidly being destroyed, but fell in late September until the ClO could no longer be detected in early October, at around the time the ozone depletion stopped. For comparison, abundances of ClO 9 to 12 miles above North America are typically around 0.01 ppb. As the icing on the cake, the SUNY observations showed that the abundance of ClO over Antarctica rose during the morning, peaked at midday, declined in the evening, and was undetectable at night, exactly as expected if it was being produced by chemical reactions involving ozone and stimulated by sunlight. The obvious place for the ClO to go during the night would be into chlorine dioxide—just the compound that Susan Solomon's group had detected in such large quantities.

It wasn't, however, all plain sailing for the chemists. Philip Solomon's team also found surprisingly low concentrations of nitrous oxide in the atmosphere above Antarctica—so low, in fact, that they could not measure it at all during most of September and October 1986.

Presenting their results at the spring meeting of the American Geophysical Union, in Baltimore, Maryland, in May 1987, Solomon pointed out that since all previous theoretical models of the chemistry of the Antarctic stratosphere had assumed "normal" concentrations of nitrous oxide (and, indeed, of other chemicals), "none of the models of Antarctica are really correct." In spite of this evidence that something very strange, chemically speaking, goes on in the Antarctic stratosphere each spring, some diehards refused to accept that chemistry really was the driving force for the ozone destruction—which perhaps is why, when the SUNY team published their results in *Nature* in July 1987, they stressed in their final sentence that these observations "leave little doubt that the development of the Antarctic ozone hole involves chlorine chemistry as a direct and prominent feature." That comment appeared on July 30, 1987; what "little doubt" remained was to be dispelled within the next two months.

SOUTH FROM PUNTA ARENAS

Punta Arenas, at the tip of South America, is the southernmost city in the world. One of its main contacts with the outside world, apart from a few tourists attracted by its rugged surroundings, is through its role as a staging post for flights into Antarctica in support of the scientific bases established there. It has a major airport with three large runways, but the city of 100,000 people had never experienced anything like the influx of scientists that arrived in August 1987. Quick work by NASA had succeeded in putting together an international mission to investigate the ozone hole—the Airborne Antarctic Ozone Experiment. Although NASA took the lead in organizing and managing the project (a direct benefit from its involvement in the CFC controversy of the 1970s), the National Science Foundation, the National Oceanographic and Atmospheric Administration, and the U.S. Chemical Manufacturers Association were also substantially involved in the project. Universities and government research establishments in the United States, Britain, Argentina, Chile, and France contributed their expertise and personnel, while Argentina, Chile (in which Punta Arenas is sited), and New Zealand provided support facilities. The experiment cost between $10 million and $20 million, directly, without making any allowance for the development costs of the instruments. It centered on two aircraft, laden with scientific instruments (twenty-one experiments in all) that flew off southward repeatedly during the Southern Hemisphere spring of 1987, probing into the hole over Antarctica at two different altitudes.

One of the aircraft, a converted DC-8 airliner, carried a team of scientists as well as instruments (up to forty people, including the flight crew) on a series of flights at an altitude of around 7.5 miles, at the bottom of the ozone layer. It was the other aircraft, however, that caught the public's imagination and gained most attention in the publicity for the Airborne Antarctic Ozone Experiment. This was an ER-2, a research version of Lockheed's famous U-2 spy plane. Although the design dates from the 1950s, the updated version of the U-2 is still one of the best aircraft around when it comes to making very high altitude flights—but it is a single-seater, single-engined aircraft, not originally designed to carry much in the way of payload. Scientific instruments for the ER-2 flights, which were shared by three pilots, were packaged in two pods, one under each wing, and operated automatically once they were switched on by the pilot. The aircraft flew at altitudes of about 12.5 miles, right in the heart of the region where balloon flights had shown the most ozone depletion.

This is virtually the limit of the heights that can be reached by jet aircraft; to go any higher, you need a rocket-propelled spaceship. The thin air and extreme cold at these altitudes meant that there was a real risk involved in making such flights, especially in a single-engined aircraft where one thing going wrong can prove fatal. Both the scientists and the pilots involved in the mission prefer to play down the risks; there was a job that needed doing, and the pilots did it. Still, their contribution to the success of the Airborne Experiment should be acknowledged.

While the ER-2 instruments made their measurements only on air samples from the immediate vicinity of the aircraft, some of the DC-8 instruments, with human operators at their controls, probed upward into the high stratosphere, using variations of the remote sensing techniques used at ground stations. Instruments on board the ER-2 measured ozone concentrations, aerosol particles, water, chlorine monoxide, bromine monoxide, nitrogen oxides, and nitric acid in the vicinity of the aircraft, at altitudes ranging from about 7.5 miles to a little over 11 miles. Instruments carried on the DC-8 also measured ozone, aerosol particles, and water near the aircraft, plus the distribution of ozone in the 6 miles *above* the aircraft, and the total column of ozone overhead; other DC-8 packages recorded total column amounts for the part of the atmosphere above the aircraft for chlorine nitrate ($ClONO_2$), chlorine dioxide ($OClO$), bromine monoxide, NO and NO_2, hydrochloric acid, and nitric acid, among other substances. Both aircraft, of course, provided measurements of temperatures in the stratosphere.

Altogether, the ER-2 made twelve sorties down to about latitude 72° S, the limit of its 3,500-mile range, with a flying time of six to eight hours on each mission. The DC-8 made twelve return flights much deeper into the air over Antarctica, and finished the expedition by flying across the Antarctic continent and on to New

Zealand, taking measurements all the way. Back at the NASA-Goddard Space Flight Center, researchers dropped everything else for the duration of these missions to process the data from TOMS, on *Nimbus 7*, and other satellite experiments almost as fast as they came in—in real time, instead of taking months to analyze the data, as is routine. Other satellites, both European and American, made observations to coincide with the Airborne Experiment, but with instant pictures of the ozone hole, the TOMS team was able to tell the group at Punta Arenas where to direct the two aircraft in order to make the best measurements of ozone depletion.

Scientists on the ground were also active during August and September 1987, and on into October. A second expedition to McMurdo, NOZE II, provided follow-up studies to those of the previous year, and coordinated ground-based observations to match up with the aircraft data, while observations continued at Halley Bay, the South Pole, and other scientific stations. At Punta Arenas, the group of researchers included theorists, brought along so that they could work on the data as they came in and develop an improved understanding of the mechanisms of ozone depletion on the spot.

Usually, with a major scientific study of this kind, it might take months to analyze all the data, and scientific papers reporting conclusions based on the observations would appear a year or more after the event. But NASA's Bob Watson, in charge of the mission, appreciated both the importance of the new observations for political decision-making and the widespread public interest and concern about the hole over Antarctica. Although some of the air samples had yet to be taken back to research laboratories in the United States and elsewhere for analysis, and though the detailed interpretation of other data would still have to be carried out at slightly more leisure, the expedition organizers held a press conference in Washington on September 30,

1987—just days after the completion of the mission—to announce their most important immediate findings. They also promised that a full report would be issued in six months, in April 1988. But since the analysis at the end of September 1987 was, of necessity, very much a preliminary first cut at the problem, the scientists insisted that only broad outlines and major conclusions would be presented then, and that detailed breakdowns with precise numbers would have to await the April 1988 report. Until then, only scientists involved in the mission had access to the data—and scientists involved in any one experiment could, if they wished, keep their own data to themselves, not even sharing it with colleagues involved in other experiments on the same flights, until they had double-checked everything and made sure of their conclusions.

Even with these understandable restrictions, the September 30 announcement established beyond doubt the role of chlorine from CFCs in destroying ozone over Antarctica. No scientific effort on this scale, and probably none on any lesser scale, had ever been interpreted and made public so quickly, and there is now no excuse for further political delays and inaction, since the scientific evidence is unambiguous.

The fruits of six weeks of flying over a total of more than 110,000 miles were summed up by Bob Watson at the end of September. The region of the ozone hole is extremely low in water (dehydrated) and in nitrogen compounds (denitrified), while almost every chemical species suspected of being involved in the destruction of ozone was present in abnormal concentrations—either far too much, or far too little, compared with measurements made at lower latitudes. For chlorine monoxide, the Punta Arenas group was prepared to put some numbers into their preliminary report—they confirmed Phil Solomon's ground-based measurements from 1986, indicating concentrations of a few parts per billion in the hole. Hydrochloric acid, important because chlorine locked up in the acid is *not* available to react with ozone, was present only in "very low" concentrations, while the concentration of nitrogen oxides inside the hole was only in the range from 0.5 to 4 ppb, compared with 8 to 12 ppb outside the hole. Bromine monoxide was found, but only in concentrations of a few parts per trillion (ppt), suggesting that it was not the major cause of ozone depletion. But the ER-2 pilots reported flying through extensive cloud cover, even at an altitude of about 11.5 to 12.5 miles. PSCs were not just present, they stretched across the sky, while instead of the stratosphere being warmer at these altitudes, as it should be if ozone were present absorbing ultraviolet energy, temperatures dropped to −130 degrees F at about 12.5 miles altitude, low enough to prevent the aircraft from flying any higher for fear that its fuel would freeze.

All this should be set against the background of satellite and ground-based measurements, plus balloon data, which showed that the destruction of ozone over Antarctica in the spring of 1987 was more pronounced than ever before—the "hole" was the deepest yet. The concentrations of ozone in the total column overhead between latitudes 70° and 80° S were about 15 percent lower than in 1985, the previous greatest depletion, and more than half the ozone in the hole was destroyed. The depletion was far worse at the critical altitudes. At Halley Bay, 76° S, balloon flights showed that on October 7, just after the Airborne Experiment ended, 97.5 percent of the ozone that had been present at 10.3 miles altitude on August 15 had gone. "Ozone," said Farman in his *New Scientist* article, "was virtually undetectable at this height." Data from the Punta Arenas expedition indicated where it had gone.

The ER-2 flights in particular showed that the region of dehydrated and denitrified air was maintained inside a sharply defined region, what Watson described as a "kind of containment vessel," and that within this region there were very low values of F-11, F-12, CH_3CCl_3,

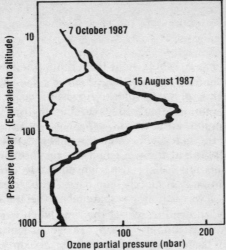

and N_2O. The implication is that the high-altitude air in the region had received a long exposure to solar ultraviolet radiation, possibly at even higher altitudes as it has moved from lower latitudes to the pole, so that the anthropogenic chlorine compounds have been broken down. It is, in a sense, very "old" air. It had then sat through the polar night, with no sunlight to trigger photochemical reactions, while water and nitrogen compounds had been locked up in the PSCs, leaving the chlorine free to do its photochemical work when the Sun returned. The key observation reported at the briefing is that there was a very close correlation (strictly speaking, an anticorrelation) between the measured concentrations of ozone and of chlorine monoxide. Ozone was least where chlorine monoxide was greatest, and there was enough ClO at around 11.25 miles altitude to explain completely the observed depletion of ozone. No numbers were placed on this correlation at that briefing; but it was a theme to which Watson would return, with marginally more detailed information, at the Dahlem workshop a few weeks later.

THE DAHLEM DEBATE

The Dahlem workshop, held in Berlin in the first week of November 1987, brought together some familiar names in the ozone story. Lovelock, Rowland, and Crutzen, involved from the early days in the 1970s; Farman, Philip Solomon, and Watson, associated with the investigation of the hole over Antarctica; and others besides. The atmosphere at the workshop was the most scientifically stimulating I have experienced. Only one other time in my life remotely compares with it. Twenty years ago, I was a junior researcher at the Institute of Astronomy, in Cambridge, at the time when colleagues in the radio astronomy group discovered pulsars. At that time, there was only one topic of conversation among the astronomical community, over coffee, at lunchtime, or driving home in the evening. Scientific history was being made, and everyone involved knew it; many senior colleagues told me how lucky I was to experience this once-in-a-lifetime event and that many researchers could live out their lives without participating in anything so exciting. Now, here I was, if only as an observer, sharing in a second "once-in-a-lifetime" scientific development, with the added awareness that this time the subject under discussion wasn't something of abstract interest to astronomers and physicists alone, but a problem that affected literally every living thing on the surface of the Earth.

Although they did not express it that way, the participants in the workshop shared the sense of urgency that implies. It was a time for jackets to be doffed and shirtsleeves rolled up. The program for the meeting, for example, allotted the first morning for the team members in each specialist group to take stock of the problem they had been assigned and sort out a plan of campaign for the rest of the week. This took the ozone team about ten minutes, and then the group got right in to item number one. At the end of the morning, when all the conference participants met in plenary session to consider their timetables, a solid morning's work on stratospheric ozone had already been completed.

The tone set by that first morning was maintained throughout the week. Scientific differences were aired, and cherished theories were tested to the limit against the new data from the Airborne Experiment before finally being rejected. Atmospheric modelers who had advocated the role of dynamics in creating the ozone hole, for example, looked for any possible loophole to keep those models alive. But this was not in a spirit of "my theory right or wrong"; rather, the experts seemed genuinely concerned to ensure that every possible alternative was ruled out before making a statement that chemistry, and in particular chlorine chemistry related to CFCs, was the cause of the growth of the hole in the ozone layer. This caution means that the ultimate conclusions reached by the team carry that much more weight than they might have done without the cut and thrust of such a debate. In the same spirit, wild ideas were sometimes aired—could it be that something totally new and previously unthought of was responsible? But nothing stood up to the heat of the debate. As the week passed, all other possibilities were eliminated during the discussions among these experts from different scientific disciplines.

Their debates were lively and, ultimately, authoritative. By the end of the week, although it was obvious that many details of the mechanisms involved still had to be worked out, and would keep both chemists and dynamicists busy for the months and years ahead, it was established that chlorine from industrial products, especially CFCs, is chiefly to blame for the destruction of ozone in Antarctic spring. This discovery alone justifies the effort and the cost of the recent missions to Antarctica, and provides a basis for action. Although the detailed mechanisms involved require much more investigation, it seems appropriate also to outline here the present understanding of the dynamics and chemistry involved, with the proviso that this is by no means the final word.

As the leader of the Airborne Experiment, Bob Watson, in particular, had seen a wealth of the data gathered on the flights from Punta Arenas. He was honor bound not to disclose any details that had not already been made public at the press conference on September 30—not even to other scientists engaged in the study of the ozone hole. But he was allowed to show those assembled in Berlin one piece of evidence that alone clinches the link between ozone depletion and CFCs. Measurements made at 11.5 miles altitude as the ER-2 crossed the boundary into the region of ozone destruction—the edge of the "chemical containment vessel"—show a steep rise in the concentration of ClO, from amounts up to 10 times greater than those found at lower latitudes to concentrations 500 to 1,000 times greater than those at lower latitudes. Over exactly the same few miles of the aircraft's flight path, the concentration of ozone was halved. Watson had been permitted, by Jim Anderson, the experimenter who made these observations (but who was not present at the Berlin gathering), to bring along to the meeting a couple of graphs plotting the changes in concentrations of ozone and chlorine monoxide as the aircraft flew south. The two curves mirror each other almost exactly, with ClO rising where O_3 falls; and when Watson showed the second plot, giving details over a smaller distance-scale (essentially a magnification of the most interesting region of the first graph), we could see that virtually every little wiggle in one line was mirrored by a corresponding wiggle, in the opposite direction, in the other line.

Anderson had given permission for the plots to be presented in Berlin, but not for them to be copied; and since this book was published before the Spring 1988 meeting at which the data from the Punta Arenas flights were made public, I am not allowed to reproduce them here. Nobody who has seen the figures, though, could doubt their import. People talk of finding the "smoking gun" that incriminates CFCs; this is more in the nature of a signed and witnessed confession. Whatever it was that was taking ozone out of the stratosphere involved chlorine monoxide in the right quantities and in the same place, at the same time.

On all flights, the correlation was clear, although sometimes the transition across the edge of the containment vessel was less clear-cut than on others. Anderson's data showed, however, that although the edge of the circumpolar vortex, the circular wind pattern cutting Antarctic air off from the outside world in winter and early spring, was at about 60° S, the edge of the chemically perturbed region—the containment vessel—was between 65° and 68° S. The ozone hole is smaller than the circumpolar vortex, and much more closely related, in 1987 at least, to the boundaries of the Antarctic continent—something for the theorists to puzzle over when they tackle the details of the mechanisms that deplete ozone in the region, but not a discovery that casts any doubt on the connection between ClO and ozone depletion. Armed with all the available data from 1987, as well as with the observations from 1986 and previous years, the group gathered in Berlin was able to make a good stab at suggesting how the mechanism works.

The ozone hole itself lies within the polar vortex, but there are smaller changes in stratospheric ozone that extend out to about 45° S. The main destruction of ozone measured in 1987 was between 9 and 15 miles altitude, overlapping with the range affected in 1986, but slightly higher. As yet, nobody knows whether this is a significant change or whether the 1986 measurements may be slightly inaccurate. There are changes in other seasons, as well as spring, so that the total amount of ozone in the polar stratosphere averaged over the whole year has been in decline since about 1979.

Although the main hole in the ozone layer is more or less centered on the South Pole, during August 1987 smaller features, dubbed "miniholes," appeared just outside the region of polar night. Each minihole lasted for a few days and then disappeared, but by mid-September several miniholes appeared at the same time, and then merged into a larger region depleted in ozone. Nobody knows whether these holes, which seem to come from higher latitudes and could very well be related to the movement of air masses licking down into the deeper south, help to create the main hole, or whether they are a related but independent phenomenon. There is still a great deal of work to be done to find out exactly what is going on in the Southern Hemisphere atmosphere. But when it comes to outlining the mechanisms at work inside the polar vortex, the models begin to hang together.

The evidence for what Watson calls "incredibly low" concentrations of F-11 and F-12 in the stratospheric air inside the "chemical containment vessel" helps to establish that this is very old air that is arriving from high altitudes after a long exposure to solar ultraviolet, and this helps to rule out the possibility that the hole is caused by the dynamic influence of rising air masses pushing ozone out of the region. The fact that the CFCs have been broken down also, of course, provides a definite source for the chlorine implicated in the chemical processes of ozone destruction—but to anyone not versed in the photochemical subtleties, it also raises the question of why the destruction has to wait for Antarctic spring. If there is plenty of chlorine around, why doesn't it do its work everywhere, all the time?

The reason is that under the normal conditions that prevail in most of the stratosphere, most of the time, a great deal of the chlorine is tied up in other compounds. Chlorine reacts with other chemicals in the air, including water and various nitrogen compounds, and becomes locked up in reservoirs such as HCl and $ClONO_2$. Chlorine monoxide, in particular, will rapidly be converted into chlorine nitrate $(ClONO_2)$ by oxides of nitrogen. Once chlorine is in these compounds, it may not be as securely locked up as in CFCs, but is still not immediately available to react with ozone. Some free chlorine is indeed available to scavenge ozone, and this is what is allowed for in the standard calculations of the global influence of CFCs on the stratosphere. But— and it is a scary thought in light of what has happened over Antarctica recently—there is a lot more chlorine potentially available, if it can be released from these other compounds. The problem over Antarctica seems to be that during the long polar night, chemical processes that, as far as we know, occur naturally nowhere else on Earth, take chlorine atoms out of these reservoirs and release them. They then have little effect on ozone until the spring, when sunlight returns and photochemical processes begin to work.

The key to this release of chlorine from reservoir molecules is the very low temperature of the winter stratosphere over Antarctica, which allows polar stratospheric clouds to form. The PSCs were named, and became the subject of scientific investigation, only in the satellite age. But Antarctic explorers going back to the pioneers in the early part of this century have reported seeing high clouds, still lit by sunlight even after the onset of the long winter night; so it is certain that PSCs were around, in some form, long before we had satellites to study them. It is possible, however, that the nature of these clouds has changed recently, at least in the Antarctic, because of the cooling of the stratosphere.

Some of the latest calculations, including those by Crutzen and Arnold, suggest that the particles in the PSCs are formed out of nitric acid and water, not out of water alone. At temperatures above about −108 degrees F (that is, 195 degrees above absolute zero, or 195 K), the clouds form as a haze of liquid droplets. Small ice particles form as the temperature drops below this value, and at temperatures below −117 degrees F (190 K), the "frost point," the cloud particles are larger, icy mixtures of frozen water and nitric acid.* This has two effects. First, the surfaces of the particles provide a place where chemical reactions that release chlorine gas can take place. Second, at the colder temperatures larger particles form—perhaps as "big" as .0003 of an inch across— and these can fall down through the stratosphere at a rate of about 1.25 miles a week, carrying the water and nitric acid away. Detailed calculations show that the effects not only depend critically on temperature (explaining why the ozone destruction could have been triggered suddenly in the late 1970s), they restrict the activity to a layer of the atmosphere between 6 and 15 miles altitude, exactly as observed.

All this freezing and chemical preconditioning of the stratosphere takes time as well as low temperatures. In the Arctic, temperatures do not fall quite so low, and the polar vortex is less pronounced, so there is no long-lived, stable region of still air in which these chemical processes can go on. The special conditions over Antarctica are exactly the right conditions to precondition the stratospheric chemistry in the right way. And it is certainly possible that a key contribution to the cool-

---

*Freezing occurs at these low temperatures, instead of at 32 degrees F (273 K) because of the low pressure high in the atmosphere.

ing of the Antarctic stratosphere that has triggered this process may have come from the greenhouse effect, trapping heat closer to the ground.

This preconditioning chemistry involves mixtures of gases, liquids, and solids, and the rates at which reactions occur under such "heterogeneous" conditions are still being investigated in laboratories around the world. It is far harder to get an understanding of these reactions than it is if all the compounds are present as a homogeneous mixture of gases. As a further complication, just as substances can be dissolved in liquids to make solutions, so some of the compounds involved are mixed into the solid particles of water ice or nitric acid ice, as "solid solutions." Studies carried out by Mario Molina show that a solid solution of hydrochloric acid (HCl) in water ice, for example, might, under polar stratospheric conditions, contain a few percent HCl molecules scattered through the crystal lattice of the ice. Chemists such as Molina have only just begun to measure the rates at which the appropriate reactions occur on the surfaces of actual ice particles at the appropriate temperatures in the laboratory, but they already have strong evidence that two key processes will be at work in the frozen polar stratospheric clouds over Antarctica in winter.*

---

*Just after this chapter was written, the November 27, 1987 issue of *Science* carried reports from two groups of scientists based in California, confirming the importance of these reactions. Researchers at SRI International, Menlo Park, and at NASA's Jet Propulsion Laboratory, Pasadena, had recreated in sealed vessels in their laboratories the conditions that exist in PSCs in the lower Antarctic stratosphere in winter. They mixed chlorine nitrate and water with the ingredients of PSCs—ice mixed with nitric acid and sulfuric acid. The compounds produced by the resulting chemical reactions included HOCl and nitric acid droplets, as well as chlorine monoxide. The reactions took place in a few thousandths of a second.

$ClONO_2$(surface) + HCl(solid solution) → Cl_2(gas) + HNO_3(surface)
$ClONO_2$(surface) + H_2O(ice) → HOCl (gas) + HNO_3 (surface)

Other, similar reactions (including some involving bromine) are thought to take place on the surfaces of the icy crystals in the PSCs, but this is sufficient to give you the broad picture. Simply removing nitric acid (HNO_3) from the gases in the atmosphere, by freezing it, will also directly influence the release of chlorine from hydrochloric acid. Molecules of nitric acid are very effective at removing OH (hydroxyl) from the stratosphere, but if the nitric acid has frozen out, the amount of OH can build up. When that happens, it reacts with hydrochloric acid instead, releasing chlorine:

$$OH + HCl → H_2O + Cl$$

Measurements in the region of ozone depletion do, indeed, show very low concentrations of HCl.

Whatever its exact origin, once active chlorine is released from reservoirs such as $ClONO_2$ and HCl, which are the most abundant "stores" for Cl in the lower stratosphere in other parts of the world, ozone scavenging can occur very efficiently—once the sunlight returns. In one cycle, for example,

$$Cl + O_3 → ClO + O_2$$
$$OH + O_3 → HO_2 + O_2$$
$$ClO + HO_2 → HOCl + O_2$$
$$HOCl + UV → OH + Cl$$

The first steps occur even without sunlight, and ClO and HOCl build up during the Antarctic winter; but the key step is the effect of solar ultraviolet, which returns OH and CL to scavenge more ozone molecules; the net effect of this cycle is:

$$2O_3 → 3O_2$$

and each chlorine atom can go around the loop tens of thousands of times.

This cycle alone cannot account for all of the spring-time ozone depletion, but it is not alone. Another powerful ozone-eating cycle also begins with the familiar simple reaction:

$$Cl + O_3 \rightarrow ClO + O_2$$

Any two molecules of ClO produced in this way can then interact, in the presence of some other molecule M:

$$ClO + ClO + M \rightarrow Cl_2O_2 + M$$
$$Cl_2O_2 + UV \rightarrow Cl + ClOO$$
$$ClOO + M \rightarrow Cl + O_2 + M$$

Once again, the overall effect is:

$$2O_3 \rightarrow 3O_2$$

and chlorine has been returned to the beginning to repeat the process. The form of chlorine dioxide that appears in this reaction has chlorine on one end of the molecule, and is not the same as OClO. The whole cycle proceeds efficiently only if there is enough ClO around, but the measurements made by Phil Solomon's team show so much ClO at 12.5 miles (about one part per billion) that *all* of the ozone depletion at that level could be accounted for by this mechanism.

Nobody would yet claim to have all the answers to the ozone depletion process, but there is clearly no difficulty in accounting for ozone destruction once Cl and ClO are present and the Sun is above the horizon. McElroy's attempt to get bromine back on center stage, however, does not seem to have succeeded. Although there is a cycle

$$Cl + O_3 \rightarrow ClO + O_2$$
$$Br + O_3 \rightarrow BrO + O_2$$
$$BrO + ClO \rightarrow Br + Cl + O_2$$

with the net effect

$$2O_3 \rightarrow 3O_2$$

The measured abundances of BrO, only a few parts per trillion at 11.5 miles altitude, show that this can be contributing only about 10 percent of the overall destruction of ozone in the hole over Antarctica.

Everything hangs together, implicating chlorine and ClO in the development of the hole (although there is very little ClO below about 10 miles altitude, and more studies of the chemistry and dynamics of the lower stratosphere are needed to explain what is going on there). Dynamical changes (perhaps, though not definitely, linked with the greenhouse effect) have set up a cold vortex over Antarctica where icy PSCs form in winter, and chemistry then does the rest. Ozone is destroyed chemically in late August and early September each year, and then recovers from October onward (though not to the concentrations of the mid-1970s) as the PSCs evaporate and the chemical conditions return to the normal state of the stratosphere elsewhere in the world. And although a dynamical change may have set up the special conditions that allow the chemistry to get to work, the consequences for Antarctic ozone would not have been anywhere near as great if there were not a large and increasing amount of chlorine getting into the stratosphere as a result of human activities, especially the release of CFCs to the atmosphere. A cold, still "containment vessel" laced with frozen PSCs may have formed many times in past decades, when the winters happened to be particularly cold; but never before were there anthropogenically produced chlorine compounds around to take advantage of these conditions. As long as Antarctica is the only region affected, this may only be a cause of mild concern. But will Antarctica be the only region affected?

CHAPTER SEVEN

GLOBAL IMPLICATIONS

The fact that the Antarctic ozone hole is not just an isolated phenomenon is shown by the extent of ozone depletion over the Southern Hemisphere in recent years. TOMS data, and other measurements, show that there has been a reduction in ozone right out to 45° S, to the southern tips of South America, Australia, and New Zealand. In the past couple of years, springtime measurements of stratospheric ozone at the latitude of southern New Zealand have shown reductions by as much as 20 percent below the values that were measured before 1979. This is far outside the containment vessel that marks the boundary of the hole proper, and suggests that other influences related to the changed dynamics of the Southern Hemisphere, and the stratospheric cooling, may be at work outside the hole.

DILUTION DYNAMICS

The hole itself could contribute to the decline in ozone concentrations across the Southern Hemisphere. The overall "lifetime" of ozone in the lower stratosphere is about a year, which means that any disturbance of ozone concentrations, a decrease or an increase, is "remembered" for about that long. Each year, large quantities of air very low in ozone may be moving out of Antarctica and mixing in the general circulation of the winds of the Southern Hemisphere, once the polar vortex breaks down in early summer. If it takes more than a year for the lost ozone to be rebuilt by photochemistry at lower latitudes, then there will be a carryover effect accumulating from year to year, until a new balance is struck with the rate at which ozone is being produced.

It's a bit like having a bath being filled by water from a tap and drained from a hole in the bottom at the same time. The higher the level of water in the bath, the faster it squirts out of the hole, because of the excess pressure; so the level of water in the bath will settle to a constant height as long as the inflow and outflow are in balance. But if the hole in the bottom is made slightly bigger, at first the level in the bath will fall, as more water escapes. As it does so, the pressure reduces and the outward flow slows, until it is once again just sufficient to balance the inflow. The level has fallen to a new stable position, even though the inflow has not changed. According to Mahlman, the dilution effect could produce an overall decline in ozone concentrations of the Southern Hemisphere stratosphere of 3 or 4 percent if the Antarctic hole becomes a permanent springtime feature.

This is not a disastrous drop in ozone concentrations in itself, but would add to any long-term, gradual decline caused by the effects of chlorofluorocarbons and other chlorine compounds (and, indeed, to any NO_x effects from SSTs or other sources) at middle latitudes. To put it in perspective, it is about what the efforts at reducing CFC releases enshrined in the Montreal agreement would save, if they came into full force. The hole over Antarctica alone could already have undone all the benefits of the Montreal agreement.

WORLDWIDE DEPLETIONS

If it had not been for the discovery of the Antarctic ozone hole, however, there would still have been plenty to worry about in 1986 and 1987. Measurements from the Solar Backscatter Ultraviolet instrument on *Nimbus* 7, reported by Donald Heath and his colleagues at Goddard, show a dramatic *overall* decline in the concentration of stratospheric ozone around the globe. The total ozone measured by SBUV stayed much the same from the time the satellite was launched in 1978 until 1982. Then, the concentrations fell, recovered a little, and plunged again in 1984 and 1985. Over a period of seven years, the total ozone content of the stratosphere declined by 4 percent, if these figures can be taken at face value. But can they?

All satellite observations suffer from the problem that nobody can take a look at the instruments in orbit to make sure they are continuing to perform properly. The instruments "drift" as they deteriorate and age, and it is difficult to recalibrate them (for example, by comparison with observations made from ground stations) to be sure that the numbers mean what they say. Ironically, in recent years some ground stations that used to monitor things like stratospheric ozone have actually been shut down, as an economy measure, on the grounds that satellites are so much better at the job that ground stations are no longer needed. In truth, the best overview of stratospheric ozone comes from a combination of satellites and an effective worldwide network of ground stations. We need more ground stations, not fewer, if we are to understand why the ozone layer is changing so swiftly.

Meanwhile, Heath's SBUV data have been treated with extreme caution and are still not accepted as gospel. But they seem to be telling us that the depletion of stratospheric ozone has lately been going on twice as fast as could be accounted for by adding in the effects of everything from CFCs and nitrous oxide to solar activity. At least one set of ground data, obtained by James Angell, of the National Oceanographic and Atmospheric Administration, confirms the trend—a decline of 4 percent in total ozone between 1980 and 1985. There may be uncertainties about the size of the trend, but every indicator available reports that global stratospheric ozone is on the decrease, and the rate looks to be as high as half a percentage point per year.

Some of this may, indeed, be due to changes in the Sun. When solar activity is at a peak, as it was in 1979, there is more ultraviolet radiation, which promotes the photochemical production of stratospheric ozone. As the Sun has now (1988) just passed through the minimum phase of its cycle of activity, over the next few years this part of the effect should reverse, slowing or even halting the decline in ozone concentrations. Indeed, it is possible that effects related to changing solar activity may have helped to establish the special conditions over Antarctica that have allowed the hole to grow so much, so soon—even though they are not the dominant mechanism of ozone destruction in the hole. If these influences reverse in the next few years, the problem of the hole over Antarctica may seem to diminish, temporarily. That could be unfortunate, if it encourages scientists and politicians to think that the problem has gone away. The true implication would be that in the middle 1990s, when the Sun is next in decline and the containment vessel is fully reestablished, there will be an even more dramatic growth of the ozone hole, because of all the additional chlorine from CFCs that will have reached the southern stratosphere by then.

The ozone loss reported by SBUV is not spread evenly across the globe, but is concentrated at high northern and southern latitudes in both spring and fall. It also occurs at higher altitudes than does the development of the hole over Antarctica—averaged over the entire globe, at an altitude of almost 25 miles, 12 percent of the ozone disappeared between 1978 and 1984, if the data are correct. This could be significant. Although a great deal of chlorine is tied up in chlorine nitrate at altitudes from about 7.5 to 20 miles (except, as we have seen, in the circumpolar vortex during the Antarctic winter night), above 20 miles chlorine nitrate is itself broken down by solar ultraviolet to release chlorine and ClO. It is just the altitude where the anthropogenic effect from CFCs and other chlorine compounds should begin to be observed—although nobody predicted that the effect would be this big, this quickly.

A NORTHERN HOLE?

Perhaps the most contentious, and frightening, of Heath's claims, however, is the discovery—if that is what it is—of a small polar hole in the ozone layer over the Arctic. The north polar stratosphere usually stays a crucial 18 degrees F or more warmer than the Antarctic stratosphere, and if freezing out of nitric acid is a crucial step in the creation of the Antarctic hole, then there should be no northern counterpart. But there are PSCs over the Arctic, so nitric acid is at least being produced in the liquid form, and that may relate to Heath's SBUV observations. Even then, there are problems. Because of the different dynamics of wind patterns in the Northern Hemisphere, compared with the Southern, the temperature over the polar region increases at the end of winter as warm air pushes in from lower latitudes. There is no strong circumpolar vortex to prevent this, and as a result the PSCs evaporate before the Sun returns. In that case, the chemistry ought to be back to normal, and no ozone depletion should occur. But that same variability of northern winds means that it is possible for the weaker northern polar vortex, complete with PSCs, to be pushed bodily off the pole and out into sunlit regions at the end of winter, before the clouds have evaporated. So, maybe, some photochemical depletion of ozone *is* possible. It will certainly be interesting and informative to find out whether any small regions of cold, still air over the Arctic do suffer ozone loss in late winter. *Maybe* that is what Heath is seeing.

The decline in ozone he measured over north polar regions in the early 1980s is less than the amount measured by the same instruments at the South Pole in those years; it covers a shallower region; and it extends over only one-third of the area of the Antarctic hole. But since it lies over populated regions of the globe, including most of Norway, Sweden, and Finland, the implications for human beings could be more immediate. Partly as a result of these measurements, partly as a means of testing some of the ideas about the Antarctic hole, a multinational expedition is traveling to the north of Norway to take observations in the winter and spring of 1988. If they find anything to confirm Heath's claims, we may well see, in 1989, a full-blown expedition on the scale of recent investigations of the hole over Antarctica. Perhaps even the presence of PSCs containing liquid acid drops, instead of ice crystals, is enough to set in motion some of the chemical processes that lead to scavenging of ozone from the stratosphere. If so, there could be implications at lower latitudes. The Arctic expedition being mounted in the winter of 1988 is a modest affair compared with the Airborne Experiment and is being run on a limited budget. It is a pathfinding exercise, an attempt to see if there is anything going on that would justify the cost of a full-scale expedition in 1989. Even so, teams from countries including Germany, Sweden, and France, plus individual researchers from other countries, have been to the European Space Agency's rocket-launching range in the north of Sweden, at latitude 68° N, where the Sun comes up on January 15. Some of the researchers arrived in November 1987, to make observations throughout the darkest winter weeks; others set up shop for the return of the Sun itself. They have been making measurements from rockets and balloons, as well as from the ground— the observations compare with those from McMurdo in 1986, rather than with the aircraft flights of 1987 over Antarctica.

Studies of the chemical processes going on over the Arctic will provide a vital "bench mark" against which to compare the chemistry of the Antarctic stratosphere, to determine whether there is a springtime hole over the Arctic. For example, the Arctic PSCs tend to form at higher altitudes than those over Antarctica, at 12.5 to 13 miles, as well as being (almost certainly) composed of liquid drops rather than ice crystals. The members of the expedition expect, and hope, to find that there is no major Arctic hole to worry about. But by studying chemical and dynamic mechanisms different from the ones thought to be operating in the Antarctic stratosphere, they will be able to get some idea of how much ozone depletion is likely to occur at other latitudes, farther from the poles. And if they do find anything suspicious, 1989 should see an Arctic experiment to rival any of the observations yet made over Antarctica.

It is possible, though by no means proven, that similar chemical processes might operate in other parts of the world. Heterogeneous chemistry is, it seems, the key to understanding the preconditioning of the Antarctic stratosphere during the polar winter. Virtually all calculations of ozone depletion at other latitudes have so far used only homogeneous chemistry, assuming all the chemicals involved were present as gases. But there are particles around in the stratosphere, especially in a region known as the Junge layer, in the lower stratosphere. This contains tiny particles of volcanic dust, and sulfates, and the overall amount of material present at any time depends on how much volcanic activity there has been. Temperatures are also higher in the Junge layer (–63 degrees F) over most of the globe than in the region where Antarctic PSCs form (–117 degrees F). So there are small, liquid drops in the Junge layer, not frozen crystals, and they are composed of a mixture of sulfuric acid and water. Richard Turco, pointing out the possibility of a link with ozone depletion, stressed that the situation is far from identical to that of the frozen nitric acid/water particles of the Antarctic PSCs. Nevertheless, some heterogeneous processes must occur, and may speed the destruction of ozone, especially after a major volcanic eruption.

One possibility, tossed out by Ralph Cicerone at the Dahlem workshop, is that traces of metals thrown out by volcanic activity (aluminum oxide is one contender) may encourage some of the heterogeneous reactions taking place on liquid drops in the Junge layer. The South American volcano El Chichón exploded in 1982, at about the time the SBUV instrument began to detect a global decline in stratospheric ozone. This may explain the phenomenon, but it provides no comfort, since the implication is that, as over Antarctica, a combination of natural phenomena and the presence of usually high concentrations of chlorine compounds in the stratosphere is causing a much steeper decline in ozone concentrations than would happen without the anthropogenic influence. Once again, if the same kind of disturbance—in this case, a major volcanic eruption—occurs in the 1990s, when even more chlorine has reached the stratosphere, the impact will be even more pronounced.

Nobody has yet carried out a thorough investigation into the implications. But one study, by Malcolm Ko and colleagues of Atmospheric and Environmental Research, Inc., in Cambridge, Massachusetts, is, to say the least, disturbing. Ko's team ran a series of computer simulations of stratospheric chemistry using standard homogeneous reactions, and found very little impact of trace gases produced by human activities. But when they adjusted the model to take account of nonstandard chemistry, it responded by indicating a 16 percent drop in ozone concentrations by the year 2060, most of the loss occurring in the lower stratosphere. This computer simulation is a very simplistic model, of the kind described as "one dimensional," because it deals only with the vertical distribution of atmospheric components and trace gases, as if the atmosphere were the same at all geographical locations. The space in the computer that is saved by leaving out calculations of atmospheric circulation and geographical variations can be used to calculate more detailed chemistry, and it is a tradeoff, depending on just what it is you want to study, whether you use a one-dimensional model with good chemistry or a more realistic dynamic model with poor chemistry. No one, including Ko, claims that the results of his studies should be taken at face value, in isolation. But there is at least a suggestion here from the computer modelers, as well as from observations of the changing ozone concentration of the real atmosphere, that the standard models on which the most widely publicized projections of global ozone depletion are based, and which were the basis for the forecasts made at the Montreal meeting, are too optimistic by far. There is certainly more than enough here to justify severe restrictions on the release of CFC and other chlorine-containing compounds. Without going over the top into the realms of science fiction, there is also one other scary scenario that should be mentioned, just in case anyone still doubts that human activities are on a large enough scale to alter the workings of the atmosphere of our planet.

A SCARY SCENARIO

Changes in the circulation of the atmosphere over the Southern Hemisphere are now clearly implicated in establishing the conditions that allow chlorine compounds to produce a dramatic decrease in ozone concentrations over Antarctica each spring. The "worst case" scenario that might result from this would be if the depletion of ozone itself caused a strengthening of the atmospheric conditions that set up the chemical containment vessel. Such a positive feedback could change the climate of at least the Southern Hemisphere, and perhaps the whole globe, into a state that has never been experienced by human beings.

Such scare stories are usually the prerogative of the doom mongers, and are seldom backed up by reliable scientific calculations. So it was remarkable to find Jerry Mahlman, who, like Lovelock, is "not a doomwatch sort of person," setting out at the Berlin meeting the detailed case for such a change in southern climate. This is not to say that the change is certain or even likely to happen; but sober scientists are now sufficiently concerned about the scale of the changes going on in the atmosphere over Antarctica to begin calculating implications that would have seemed like science fiction even five years ago.

Mahlman's scary scenario begins with the observed fact that something—we don't know what—has caused the stratosphere at high southern latitudes to cool. Associated with this cooling, the circumpolar vortex has become more pronounced, cutting off the wintertime air high over Antarctica from the rest of the atmosphere. As a result, through the chemical processes outlined in chapter 6, ozone disappears from the Antarctic stratosphere in spring, and there is a carryover from one year to the next, with less ozone around, overall, throughout the year.

One consequence of a reduction in the ozone concentration at high altitudes is to reduce the warming influence of the Sun, because less solar ultraviolet is absorbed. So the Antarctic stratosphere *may* cool even more as a result of the ozone depletion. It may be that this feedback has helped the hole to grow each year, in the sense that more ozone is destroyed. But how cold can the core region, the containment vessel, get? So much ozone is now being destroyed each spring that in the heart of the hole this effect may have reached its limit. There is simply no more ozone to be destroyed, and the stratosphere cannot get any colder. *Perhaps* this means that the effect has reached a natural limit. Or perhaps it means that the effect is now likely to spread outward. Instead of the hole getting deeper, in the sense that more ozone is destroyed, it may get wider, extending over a broader area, to lower latitudes.

Reducing the temperature over Antarctica itself increases the stability of the polar vortex, and both increases the efficiency of the containment and pushes the circumpolar winds out to lower latitudes. Of course, the effect must be limited by the extent of the region where it becomes dark enough for long enough during the polar winter for the chemical preconditioning to occur. But it is entirely plausible, according to Mahlman, that the southern high-latitude region could "flip" into what is known as a purely radiative equilibrium state, with the steady circular winds dominating the atmospheric flow and with very little movement of air masses across latitude bands—no warm tongues of air licking down into Antarctica.

The picture is rather like the onset of a new ice age, at least in the Southern Hemisphere. In recent years, the amount of sea ice extending outward from Antarctica has increased, though not yet sufficiently for anyone to suggest that the world is entering a new ice age. Most concern about climatic change today relates to the greenhouse effect, and it is ironic that by cooling the stratosphere the greenhouse effect could be contributing to these remote, but scary, possibilities that Mahlman is drawing to our attention. It seems we have at least to consider the possibility that even a greenhouse warming of most of the globe might be associated with circulation patterns at high southern latitudes that "belong" in an ice age. Since no comparable conditions have ever been observed, the effects of this on world climate are unpredictable.

Could the effect, if it is real, spread to the Northern Hemisphere? A cooling of only 18 degrees F, perhaps a little more, of the stratosphere over the Arctic could allow the kind of icy PSCs that now form only over Antarctica to appear in the north, and if that happened there could, at the very least, be significant changes in the circulation patterns of the Northern Hemisphere.

That, however, probably does count as science fiction, even today. The slight, but real, possibility is that changes will occur in the south. Warning signs would be an expansion of the polar region covered by PSCs in winter, an increase in the contrast between relatively high ozone concentrations at lower latitudes and relatively low concentrations at higher latitudes, a decline in the overall concentration of ozone in the southern stratosphere from year to year, and an increase in the strength of the circular winds that blow around the world in fairly tightly confined latitude bands. Nobody, yet, should lose any sleep over this scenario. There is no evidence that the effect has begun to operate. Equally, though, nobody should assume that the atmosphere of the Earth is so big, and so stable, that nothing we can do can change it. On the contrary, present thinking on large-scale natural changes, such as the onset of ice ages, suggests that they occur suddenly, when the Earth passes some critical balance point during a long, slow process of gradual change.

BALANCE POINTS

Two examples, one natural, one (potentially) a result of human activities, may make the point clear. The first concerns the way ice ages begin in the Northern Hemisphere. It used to be thought that this was a long, slow process. As the Earth began to cool, the argument ran, great ice sheets would grind down out of their northern fastnesses, and glaciers would inch downward from the mountain heights. Snow falling on the embryonic ice sheets would be less likely to melt than snow falling on land or sea, so the ice sheets would get thicker year by year, and the weight of extra ice would push their edges inexorably outward. Eventually—after about fifteen thousand years—the ice could spread most of the way across a continent.

But many lines of geological evidence now show that ice ages "switch on" much more rapidly than this, in the space of a few centuries, perhaps within a hundred years, or a thousand years at most. The timing of these changes, although not the exact mechanisms that carry them through, is explained beautifully by changes in the tilt of the Earth as it orbits around the Sun. This changes the balance of heat between the seasons, so that although the average heat received by the whole globe from the Sun over the course of a year is always the same, sometimes winters are cold while summers are hot, while at other stages of the cycle summers are cool and winters are relatively mild, but still cold enough for snow to fall at the latitudes of North America and Europe. The geological evidence shows that ice age conditions are favored when summers are cool, and the alternative view of how ice ages develop explains why.

The way to make an ice age begin, it now seems, is to have snow that has fallen on land during the winter stay throughout the following summer. Snowfields are shiny and reflect away incoming solar energy. Even a very thin layer of snow can do the trick. It chills the air above it, and if it persists into the next winter it will help to ensure that any more snow that falls fails to melt. On this picture, as the balance of heat between the seasons tilts gradually in favor of cooler summers, there must come a time when *one year's* snowfall tilts the balance from interglacial to ice age conditions.

This is an extreme version of the "snowblitz" theory, as it is called. More realistically, one year's snowfall persisting through the following summer could extend the range covered by permanent snow and ice outward from the glaciers and ice sheets (in the Northern Hemisphere in particular) by dozens of miles, instead of a few inches. This advance might then be consolidated for a few years, before another step forward. A dozen such snowblitzes, in the span of a century, and the new ice age would be established.

Changes in the other direction, toward a warmer climate, could have equally dramatic effects. From time

to time, stories reporting the growth of the greenhouse
effect comment on the concern of some scientists that
there might be an "ice surge" out of Antarctica. It
seems paradoxical that warming the world might cause
Antarctic ice to spread out over the oceans, but it could
happen. The reason is that some of the ice sheets
around Antarctica extend out onto the ocean. Floating
ice sheets are no great problem. But in some places the
ice sheets that extend across the bays in the Antarctic
continent are supported by islands underneath—huge
masses of ice, not floating at all, but grounded on rocky
islands, like the roof of a great cathedral supported by
huge pillars. The weight of the ice sheet on the continent itself, sloping downward to the sea, presses down
on these grounded sheets of sea ice, trying to push
them forward. But they only inch forward, slowly,
because of the friction where they grind down on the
island pillars.

When the Earth warms, as it may now be doing
through the greenhouse effect, many glaciers around the
world begin to melt, but the Antarctic ice cap will be
the last to be affected. If anything, the Antarctic ice
sheet might grow thicker, at first, because increased
global warmth means increased evaporation at lower
latitudes, and more water vapor available in the air to
fall as snow where the world is still cold, near the poles.
At the same time, the surface layers of the oceans begin
to warm and expand. As ice melts at lower latitudes,
there is more water in the sea; as the seas warm, the
water in them expands. The effects combine to produce
a rise in sea level (and sea level has indeed been rising
worldwide throughout the twentieth century). What
does this do to the grounded ice sheets in the Antarctic
bays? As the sea level rises, these ice sheets should
begin to lift off of their supporting pillars. Water can
seep between the ice and its rocky supports—and in
those circumstances, water is an effective lubricant. At
some critical point, during a steady process of rising sea

levels, the restraining influence on the ice sheets is removed. Under the weight of ice from the Antarctic continent, the whole sheet may surge forward, calving off huge icebergs that, eventually, melt and raise sea levels still further.

There is some evidence that an ice surge of this kind may have occurred naturally, during the interglacial about 125,000 years ago. There is a possibility that something similar could happen as a result of human activities as the greenhouse effect gathers strength. Both examples—the ice surge and the snowblitz—show that conditions on Earth, especially at high latitudes in both hemispheres, can change dramatically in response to very small changes, once a slower, more steady change has reached some critical balance point. Can this be reconciled with the rather comforting idea of the stability of the Earth's ecosystem represented by the concept of Gaia?

GOODBYE TO GAIA?

The comfort provided to many people by the image of Gaia as a benevolent Earth goddess doing her best to maintain conditions on Earth just right for human life results, in fact, from a misunderstanding of what Jim Lovelock hypothesizes. His idea is that the biosphere is a self-regulating entity, which has the capacity to keep "our" planet healthy by controlling the chemical and physical environment. There is no intention here to suggest that Gaia is self-aware, any more, as Lovelock puts it, than the appelation "she" when applied to a ship means that we regard the vessel as a sentient being. Indeed, the best analogies for how Gaia may operate come from the processes that we carry out *un*consciously, with no intelligence involved at all.

In the present context, the way we maintain our body heat at, more or less, a comfortable 98.6 degrees F provides the neatest example. Lovelock is fond of describing how a combination of two different shivering processes, sweating, production of heat by burning food, and adjusting the flow of blood through vessels near the surface of our bodies combine to keep the body temperature constant even though outside temperatures may vary from 32 degrees F to above 100 degrees F. Strictly speaking (and, as it happens, appropriately), the "steady" body temperature applies only to the core of a human being, the trunk of the body and the head, where the vital organs are located. Skin, hands, and feet have to get along as best they can over a much wider range of temperatures. And it all happens automatically, without any intelligent thought involved.

Gaia, says Lovelock, operates a similar mixed bag of mechanisms to maintain a roughly stable global temperature. I'll pick out just two examples. When the Earth was young and the Sun was cooler than it is today, the atmosphere was thicker and the greenhouse effect was stronger, so surface temperatures were still high enough for liquid water to exist, and life developed in pools of liquid water. As the Sun got hotter, life was spreading and taking carbon dioxide out of the air. The greenhouse effect diminished, and the temperature of the Earth stayed much the same, without rising to the point where water boiled. Today, there is less carbon dioxide in the atmosphere, offsetting the warmer Sun. As the Sun gets warmer still, it is possible that increased biological activity, especially in the oceans, may encourage the spread of clouds. Microorganisms in the surface layers of the ocean are known to produce dimethylsulfide, DMS, which escapes into the atmosphere. DMS in the air leads to the production of particles that act as seeds, or nuclei, for cloud droplets to form. More solar energy means more DMS, which means more cloud cover and less solar energy reaching

the sea—a stabilizing, *negative* feedback, just the opposite of the kind of runaway positive feedback envisaged
in Mahlman's scary scenario. And all done, like the way
your body keeps itself warm, without any conscious
thought.

You may also wonder, if you have a mind like
Lovelock's, why the atmosphere of our planet should
contain just 23 percent oxygen, and not 15 percent, or
30 percent. A simple calculation solves the puzzle. The
principal source of oxygen in the air, says Lovelock, is
the burial of a small proportion of the carbon that is
fixed each year (out of carbon dioxide) by green plants
and algae. If all the original material decayed, all of the
carbon would be converted back into carbon dioxide.
But, because a small amount of organic carbon is buried
each year, oxygen is left over in the atmosphere and
builds up its concentration as the aeons pass. But it
cannot do so indefinitely. Oxygen is, in chemical terms,
a very hazardous element. It is only because we are so
used to it that we think nothing of breathing an atmosphere that contains 23 percent oxygen. If the stuff
had just been invented, it would be required to carry
all kinds of safety warnings, and such a high concentration (more than we need for comfortable respiration)
would surely not be permitted.

The concentration is, indeed, just at the safe upper
limit for life, and even a small increase—say, to 25
percent—would ensure that forest fires started by lightning strikes would quickly spread into raging conflagra-
tions that would engulf most of the present land vegetation, from, as Lovelock puts it, the tropical rain forests
to the Arctic tundra.

What would the effect be? Why, of course, to
reduce the amount of free oxygen in the air and to
increase the proportion of carbon dioxide! Today, forest
fires do indeed take place, but not on an all-consuming
scale. Just enough, in fact, to ensure that the oxygen
concentration of the atmosphere stays below the critical

value, and life can continue reasonably comfortably on the surface of the planet.

There are other examples, but you get the picture. Gaia regulates conditions automatically and unconsciously. "She" is not looking after us in particular. The temperature analogy is particularly apposite because, like the human body, Gaia has a core region—in the tropics and subtropical latitudes, where life proliferates and where conditions stay much the same, even during ice ages. It is only the extremities—in her case, the polar and temperate zones—that suffer extreme changes.

The doom mongers sometimes refer to the ozone layer as the weakest link in Gaia's life-support system, and up to a point they are right. But only up to a point. If the *entire* ozone layer were stripped away, it would be very bad news for us, and for most life forms that inhabit the surface of the Earth. But life would still go on in the oceans, and eventually Gaia would recover. She has, after all, recovered from comparable catastrophes in the past, such as the events, whatever they were, that led to the death of the dinosaurs 65 million years ago. *We* think that it would be a disaster if humankind were wiped off the face of the Earth. But look at it another way. Today, humankind is busily destroying the tropical forests that are the core of Gaia; we are changing the climate through the greenhouse effect; and we are destroying ozone in large quantities, at least over Antarctica. These effects add up to a disaster, for other forms of life on Earth, as great as the extinctions that occurred 65 million years ago. From the "point of view" of Gaia, the destruction of humankind might well be a good thing.

Lovelock summed up this view to me, quietly, over coffee in Berlin. "People sometimes have the attitude," he said, "that 'Gaia will look after us.' But that's wrong. If the concept means anything at all, Gaia will look after *herself*. And the best way for her to do that might well be to get rid of us." The thought is as scary as anything Mahlman was able to come up with, and reinforces the conclusion, already inescapable in light of the evidence gathered over Antarctica in 1987, that the time has come to act to protect the ozone layer.

CHAPTER EIGHT

STRATEGIES FOR ACTION

By the fall of 1987 there was no room to doubt that the problem of ozone depletion was real, immediate, and caused in large measure by the release of CFCs. In the middle of the 1970s, most scientists had been cautious about the need for action. A ban on nonessential uses of CFCs in spray cans seemed an appropriately cautious response to the questions raised by Rowland and Molina—by definition, stopping nonessential releases would not be too painful. But very few people urged any comprehensive ban on these products, since there was no direct evidence of damage to the environment. Once that evidence came in, many scientists reacted swiftly, and logically, with calls for more draconian action.

In one of a series of interviews carried out by *Omni* magazine just before the Airborne Antarctic Ozone Experiment, and published while the researchers were still in Punta Arenas, Jim Anderson, of Harvard University (one of the scientists who had an experiment on board the ER-2), said he was "shocked at the way the political community has responded to all this," and castigated politicians for ignoring the problem before the hole was discovered, then running around in "complete panic" after it was found. Referring back to the issues raised in the debate of the 1970s, when industry had argued that it was up to scientists to *prove* CFCs were harmful before their release was stopped, he went on, "As a member of the human race, I feel very strongly that chemicals are guilty until proven innocent." The point being, of course, that anything released to the environment should be subjected to the equivalent, in environmental terms, of the stringent tests for safety applied to all new drugs before they are used on the population at large. We have to be sure, you might say, that these environmental "drugs" have no adverse effect on Gaia.

In the same series of interviews, Bob Watson laid his views on the line. "If we find that ozone is decreasing in Antarctica and that it is a precursor to global ozone depletion," he was reported as saying, "then we will have to find a way to immediately get rid of CFCs for all but the most essential applications, such as refrigeration." And in the *Observer* on September 6, Joe Farman, the scientist who had found the hole over Antarctica, responded angrily to the tone of a press release that had been put out with an official UK report on the ozone layer which he had coauthored. The press release, issued by the Department of the Environment without consulting the authors of the report, had suggested that there was no great problem from CFCs, leading one newspaper headline over a story about the report to read "Sprays 'not so damaging' to ozone layer." Farman, in response, pointed out that the report said nothing of the kind, and had in fact concluded that ozone depletion could be "substantial" over a period of twenty to thirty years; but in any case, he told the *Observer*, the report had already been overtaken by new evidence, including recent studies in Antarctica, and he called for a reduction in CFC emissions by 85 percent as quickly as possible.*

My own copy of the report had, by then, been passed on to a colleague in the United States. Two days after Farman's comments appeared in the *Observer*, I tried to obtain a second copy of the report from the publishers, HM Stationery Office. It had sold out. The British public, it seemed, was more interested in, and concerned about, the problem of ozone depletion than was their government.

All this was before the ill-timed Montreal meeting. But by September 1987, scientific input to the discussions leading up to the international agreement on CFC emissions had virtually ceased. By then, the discussions were entirely in the hands of the politicians, and what was to emerge from that meeting, although at least a step in the right direction (well, nearly; one cynical commentator actually called it "a half-step"), was a masterpiece of fudge and compromise, so full of loopholes that it is hard to see just what effect it will have in the long term. To understand why such an outdated agreement appeared precisely at the time when scientists had looked at the evidence, weighed it in the balance, and come off the fence in favor of a massive reduction in CFC production, we have to go back to the dog days of the Carter administration in Washington.

---

*Not all newspapers fell into the trap. The *Guardian*, on August 7, had headlined its report "Scientists put blame for ozone gap on aerosols" (they meant spray cans, of course), and quoted Farman, as cautious and sober a scientist as you are likely to meet, as saying, "We have to make an 85 percent cut pretty sharply."

THE MONTREAL MUDDLE

In the late 1970s, the CFC problem appeared to be coming under control. Legislation in the United States had drastically cut back on spray-can uses, and in the European community there was a voluntary agreement to reduce spray-can uses by 30 percent from 1976 levels. Emissions of CFCs to the atmosphere were dropping—countries that report to the Chemical Manufacturers Association (most of the developed world except the Soviet Union) showed a decline in production of F-11 and F-12 by 26 percent between 1974 and 1982. Other uses, however, continued to grow, and in the late 1970s environmentalists tried to initiate action that would ensure that this did not undo all the good done by controlling spray-can emissions. In October 1980, the EPA outlined a proposal limiting production of CFCs in the United States to then current levels. But with the change of administration in 1981, nothing came of this. In April, 1980, however, the United Nations Environment Program (UNEP) had called on governments to reduce national use and production of CFCs. The call fell on deaf ears, but in May 1981, UNEP set up a working group of legal and technical experts, charged with the task of drafting a convention for the protection of the ozone layer. Moving at the usual pace of such committees, this working group led to the Vienna convention, which was signed by twenty countries in March 1985 (Farman's paper reporting the discovery of the hole was at that time still with *Nature*, and would not appear in print for another two months).

The convention, later signed by other countries, didn't actually say much except generalities. But it said them very nicely. In twenty-one articles, it spelled out that states had an obligation to control activities that "have or are likely to have adverse effects" on the ozone layer, and that they should cooperate on scientific investigation of the problems likely to be caused by products such as CFCs. Two technical "annexes" spelled out the kind of research and information needed; one of the few immediate tangible benefits was that in 1986 the Soviet Union released figures on CFC production for the first time.

Meanwhile, pressure for action had been building up from two groups of countries—Sweden, Norway, and Finland, acting together to urge general controls on CFCs; and the United States, Canada, and Switzerland combining to press for a ban on all spray-can uses (the Swiss became increasingly concerned in the 1980s as ground-based measurements showed a thinning of the ozone layer above their country). Workshops and discussions continued throughout 1986 and into 1987 under the UNEP umbrella. On the scientific side, these culminated in the meeting in Würzburg in April 1987. The computer models studied at that meeting suggested that holding the emissions of compounds containing chlorine or bromine to the levels projected for 1990 would produce a total column depletion of global ozone of less than 2 percent by 2050. These projections now, of course, stand out in stark contrast to the actual measurements made by Heath and Angell, and totally ignore the Antarctic hole. But they were fed into the political debate.

Far less notice was taken of the projections based on a different, and in some ways more realistic, scenario. In 1987, it was estimated that developing nations were producing one-quarter of all CFCs. The modelers in Würzburg calculated an optimistic projection first. If this production increased at 2.5 percent a year, while the developed world cut its production by half, everyone would be producing the same amount of CFCs in 2060 and the ozone depletion would then be 6 percent. The more realistic case (their choice of terminology) they discussed was a world in which only 80 percent of industrialized countries agreed to freeze production of F-11 and F-12 at 1986 levels, while the rest allowed unrestricted growth. That led to a loss of 16 percent of the ozone layer by 2060. All of these calculations are based on computer models that may or may not be accurate representations of the real world; none of them takes account of nonlinearities or heterogeneous chemistry.

The political debate, which by the spring of 1987 was gathering pace and becoming something of a slanging match, seemed to take little notice of these more gloomy predictions—although the United States, in the form of Richard Benedick, a deputy assistant secretary for the environment, slammed Britain and France for being "more interested in short-term profits than in the protection of the environment for future generations" (*New Scientist*, March 5, 1987, p. 17). By then, the United States, notably the giant Du Pont company, was the world leader in developing substitutes for CFCs, and the counteraccusation flew back that all this concern about the environment was simply a smokescreen—that America actually wanted a ban on CFCs so that they could move into the marketplace and clean up with sales of substitute. Inside Europe, however, Britain was indeed increasingly seen as out of step with the rest of the community. The European community wanted to speak with one voice at negotiations under the Vienna convention aimed at establishing a protocol restricting CFC emissions, and several European community countries expressed exasperation at Britain's refusal to countenance any cuts at all. A compromise had first to be hammered out in debate among the European countries, before their representatives could attend the UNEP meetings, where that compromise became a basis for negotiating further compromises with other countries, including the United States.

At the beginning of May 1987, when signatories to the Vienna convention met in Geneva to thrash out a draft protocol, the prospect of an effective final agreement still seemed remote. Britain was still dragging its feet, and dragging the European community (which has twelve votes in the discussions but tries to present a united front) with it. Countries such as India, South Korea, and China did not attend the meetings at all. And the compromise the nations that were involved inched toward was a wishy-washy affair involving cuts of CFC production from 1986 levels in two stages, and then only if enough nations ratified the protocol. The European community objected to the second stage of cuts, and voted for only a single cutback of 20 percent from 1986 levels (remember, a cut of 85 percent is needed simply to avoid the concentration of CFCs in the atmosphere from increasing). For two months, this looked like being the rock on which the agreement would founder; but in July, Britain suddenly changed its position to support the second round of cuts, and this enabled the European community to fall in line.

Britain's change of heart was presented at the time as a triumph for the junior environment minister, William Waldegrave, who was known to be personally concerned about the threat to the ozone layer. More cynical analysts suggested that Britain had simply been bullied into movement by the United States and West Germany, that the British government realized that it had to do something about the public image resulting from its dreadful record on environmental issues such as acid rain, and that it would cost almost nothing to restrict the use of CFCs, whereas controlling emissions of sulfur dioxide from power stations would cost billions. And a little good environmental publicity could do no harm during a general election campaign, could it?

Whatever the reasons, partly thanks to Britain's U-turn, the negotiating teams from thirty-three countries who headed for Montreal to begin, on September 8, 1987, the final round of meetings to produce a treaty to control CFC emissions had real hopes of getting something together. At that very moment, of course, the Punta Arenas missions were being flown southward over the Antarctic. After all the delays and tribulations leading up to the Montreal meeting, it is dumbfounding, to an outsider, that the meeting was not delayed for a few weeks or months to take account of the new findings. Almost as dumbfounding were the remarks made by U.S. Department of Interior Secretary Donald Hodel, reported in the first week of September as the Montreal talks were about to begin. He said that the administration should encourage Americans to wear "hats, sunglasses, and sunscreen lotion," rather than force industry to adopt substitutes for CFCs. It's that kind of remark, from that kind of politician, that almost makes you suspect that some participants were suddenly, in September 1987, eager to rush through a Montreal agreement lacking real bite, before the new data from Punta Arenas came in and pushed them into enforcing stricter restrictions.

Needless to say, there were yet more fumbles and stumbles in Montreal before the treaty was agreed. I'll spare you the details. What was eventually agreed, and signed by representatives of twenty-seven countries on September 16 (exactly two weeks before Bob Watson and his colleagues presented first results of the Airborne Experiment), ostensibly provided for a 50 percent reduction in the amount of CFCs being released (not just F-11 and F-12, but also F-113, F-114, and F-115), starting from 1986 levels. That looked good, in first reports of the agreement. And consumption of halons, widely used in fire extinguishers, is to be frozen within four years of the agreement's coming into force in 1989. All that is the good news. Study of the fine print, however, showed that there was much still to be desired. First, the controls are to come in in *three* stages. In 1990, consumption of CFCs by signatory states is to be frozen at 1986 levels. In 1994, it will be reduced by

20 percent, and later still (perhaps by 1999), trimmed by a further 30 percent of the 1986 figure. But as one of those compromises thrashed out in Montreal, *production* of CFCs is allowed to increase to 110 percent of 1986 levels by 1990, with a decrease to 90 percent of those levels in 1994, and 65 percent by 1999. The extra production is for export to developing countries, ostensibly to discourage them from building their own CFC-manufacturing plants, which would exacerbate the problem.

The treaty comes into force on January 1, 1989, assuming that by then at least eleven countries that between them control a minimum of two-thirds of global consumption of CFCs have ratified the agreement (if you're confused, blame Ronald Reagan; in an about turn as remarkable as Britain's, the United States suddenly demanded in the run up to Montreal that countries controlling 90 percent of emissions would have to ratify the treaty before it became effective; the two-thirds figure is yet another compromise). The truly astonishing achievement is that so many nations have agreed to an international treaty aimed at protecting the environment—a historic first of which Mostafa Tolba, executive director of UNEP, is justly proud. The wonder is not that it is a good treaty, but, as Dr. Johnson might have said, that it exists at all. The tragedy is that our expectations of the international political process are so low that such a feeble agreement is regarded, like a dog walking on its hind legs, as a triumph. One ray of hope is that the treaty provides for periodic reviews of the position in light of new scientific evidence. The first of these will probably be held in 1990 (though Tolba has the right to call an emergency review meeting if new evidence warrants this, and would surely be justified in doing so as soon as the Airborne Experiment data are officially published in April 1988). It is hard to see how any such meeting could now fail to tighten the terms of the Montreal agreement considerably. Though who will police the agreement, even in its present form, and bring any offenders to book, remains to be seen. Meanwhile, CFCs continue to pour into the air, and ozone continues to be attacked. Can anything be done at a more personal level?

CFCS TODAY

On the principle "know your enemy," the first thing to do is to check out just where CFCs are widely used today. Although the United States, Canada, and Sweden have banned most uses of CFCs in spray cans, in the mid-1980s this still represented about a third of the use of F-11 and F-12 worldwide, at least in the countries reporting to the Chemical Manufacturers Association, which represents some 85 percent of estimated global production. Together, the two CFCs still account for about 70 percent of all emissions, with a further 12 percent (and rapidly growing) coming from F-113, which is widely used as a solvent in the burgeoning microchip industries of countries like South Korea. F-12 is used in large quantities in the United States and Japan, in particular, as the working fluid in automobile air conditioners, and the main use of F-11 today is as a foam-blowing agent.

Quite astonishing amounts of F-12 are wasted by automobile air conditioners. In 1985, the United States produced 150,000 tons of F-12, and one-third of this went into such systems. Thirty percent of the fluid in these systems is lost by "routine" leakage, and half escapes during servicing. The rest is released when the units are eventually scrapped.

Both F-11 and F-12 are used in refrigerators, and ought to be securely sealed away there, posing no prob-

A

Estimated Use of CFC-11 by Product, 1984, U.S. and Countries Reporting to the Chemical Manufacturers Association (CMA)*

**CMA Reporting Countries
(3,306,000 tons)**   **United States
(82,650 tons)**

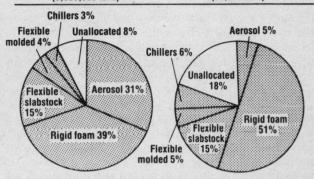

*Percentages are Estimates Reflecting Numerous Uncertainties

B

Estimated Use of CFC-12 by Product, 1984, U.S. and Countries Reporting to the Chemical Manufacturers Association (CMA)*

**CMA Reporting Countries
(402,230 tons)**   **United States
(148,770 tons)**

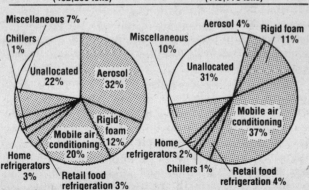

*Percentages are Estimates Reflecting Numerous Uncertainties

lem. But these units, too, are scrapped at the end of their useful lives (or when the owners get bored with them and decide to buy a new model), and then the CFCs are set free.

Although the bubbles in your Styrofoam cup or hamburger carton may contain F-11, the gas inside them is not a major threat to the ozone layer. Very little of it escapes. What is a problem is the amount of F-11 that escapes during the manufacturing process, when the plastic is foamed in the first place. This use of CFCs is rapidly expanding. Half the 83,000 tons of F-11 produced in the United States each year in the late 1980s goes into rigid foam sheets and packages (along with 11 percent of the F-12 produced), and in Britain manufacturers of so-called expanded plastic were predicting 10 percent growth in 1987.

As these examples show, there is a huge potential to reduce the amount of CFCs from getting into the atmosphere simply by making existing uses more efficient, controlling the release from factories that make foamed plastics, sealing air conditioners more effectively, and recycling the CFCs when units are scrapped. Unfortunately, CFCs are so cheap to manufacture that there has been no incentive for any of these techniques to be developed in the past. One very obvious way to provide such an incentive would be by taxing the CFCs; this could have a dual benefit if money raised in this way were spent on developing replacement chemicals.

Some overall figures (taken from the Friends of the Earth publication *Into the Void?* but originally from the Chemical Manufacturers Association reports) may put the burden of CFCs on the atmosphere in perspective. Overall, more than 700,000 tons (630 million kilograms) of F-11 and F-12 were released into the atmosphere in 1985, by which time the total amount produced but not yet released ("stored" in foams, refrigerators, and air conditioners) had reached 1,600,000 tons, almost three times the annual release. Within the European community, 370,576 tons of CFCs were produced in 1985, but this represented only 60 percent of the industry's capacity. Half as much again *could* be produced each year without building another plant—one reason why some members of the European community were so anxious to allow an increase in production from 1986 levels to provide for exports to other parts of the world. Two-thirds of this production was sold within the European community in 1985, the rest exported. Strikingly, in view of the speed with which the United States moved in the 1970s, 129,641 tons, almost 35 percent of the total, went into spray cans. Here is another area where immediate, effective action could be taken at little cost and no harm to anybody.

Taking the European community as a whole, the amount of CFCs used each year adds up to 1.8 pounds per head; in the United States, the comparable figure is 2.0 pounds, and in the whole world just 7 ounces. There, indeed, lies the heart of the problem for the future. As other countries develop further economically, they will want to use CFCs in increasing quantities. India and China, for example, with huge populations, are actively developing their refrigeration industries. It is in an attempt to recognize the need for "fair shares" that some people urge the developed world to cut its use of CFCs per head by half, while allowing the developing world to increase its consumption to the same level (the Montreal agreement does half of this, by committing signatories to a 50 percent cutback, eventually; it has no power over the speed with which nonsignatories develop their own CFC industries). It certainly is not "fair" that a small part of the total world population should have had the benefits of CFCs (such as they are) to date, but allowing fair shares for all is not going to make the depletion of the ozone layer stop. Only an immediate, permanent cutback by 85 percent will do that. It is not going to happen, unless a lot more people make a lot more noise about the problem.

LOCAL TACTICS

The Montreal agreement itself specifically says that there is nothing to prevent signatory states from taking further action to reduce CFC emissions below the levels spelled out in the protocol if they wish. The most likely reason for the government of any country to take such action will be pressure of public opinion, whether it is expressed in terms of votes, lobbying, or, as in the United States in the 1970s, by people's refusing to buy products that contain CFCs.

The obvious place to start is with spray cans. The U.S. experience has shown that life without CFC propellants is indeed possible, and as the World Resources Institute report *The Sky Is the Limit* expressed it in 1986, "each pound of CFCs currently consumed in aerosol sprays may be a pound not available for much higher valued uses in the future." Other countries should immediately follow the American lead in first labeling all cans that contain CFCs with a warning, then banning their use as propellants. Meanwhile, Friends of the Earth will happily send you, from their London office (26–28 Underwood Street, London, N1 7QT, United Kingdom) a free leaflet listing products that do not contain CFS at all. The more people make use of lists like these, the more economic pressure there will be on other manufacturers to follow suit and to reformulate their products—a completely painless process, now that the United States has led the way (don't be too complacent in North America, though; U.S. production still amounts to 30 percent of the world total, including CFCs exported for use in spray cans elsewhere in the world).

It is as important to acknowledge industries that move in the right direction as it is to castigate the ones that do not. McDonald's, the fast-food chain, secured a minor publicity coup in September 1987, at the time of the Montreal conference, by announcing its decision to change its plastic foam packages, in the United States at least, from foam made with CFCs to a foam that looks the same and keeps food just as hot, but is made with a different blowing agent. The change was to be made over eighteen months and does not, as yet, apply to McDonald's restaurants outside the United States. It may, indeed, be chiefly a publicity gimmick, but it is certainly a move in the right direction. In the electronics industry, Digital Equipment Corporation, of Andover, Massachusetts, and Salem, New Hampshire, announced in 1987 that it had already switched from cleaning processes using CFCs to a water-based system. A spokesman for the company said "we feel the consequences of underreacting are worse than the consequences of overreacting" to the ozone threat. Why can't others see the point and act accordingly?

The spread of responses even within the European community is highlighted by the contrast between Britain's foot-dragging and the situation in West Germany, where spray-can manufacturers have already agreed to cut back the use of the worst offenders, the fully halogenated CFCs, by 75 percent in 1988 and to 10 percent of 1987 levels in 1989. The reason is simply public pressure, in a country where environmental politics matter, and the Green Party is represented in government. Spray cans that do *not* contain CFCs already carry a label to that effect in West Germany, and this has been shown to increase their sales over those of rival brands.

Much of the debate on regulation and control of CFC emissions, in those countries where the problem is perceived, is now moving to the stage of discussions about mechanisms for limiting production, and whether taxes or licenses, for example, would be more effective methods of control. Would a phase-out be fairer (that word again) to manufacturers than a sudden cutback? And so on. This is simply time-wasting. What matters is that action is taken, and taken quickly. Industry always complains that it will take another five years to develop alternatives. It has been saying this since 1974, while quietly developing alternatives anyway, just in case governments decide to act. This two-handed approach was typified by two news reports in the wake of the Montreal agreement. Kevin Fay, director of the Alliance for Responsible CFC Policy, said in Washington, D.C., that "it goes much further than anything we think is necessary" (so you can guess what kind of organization that is, and what they mean by "responsible"). On the other hand, in the *European Chemical News* for October 19, 1987, you could find a story trailed on the cover with the headline "CFC producers can meet rising demand with substitutes." Inside, the story told how manufacturers, including the two giants, ICI in Britain and Du Pont in the United States, had plans to expand their production of CFC-22, a compound that poses far less risk to the ozone layer than F-11, F-12, or F-113. "Du Pont," said the report, "has recognised the potential of CFC-22 as a substitute for refrigeration, air-conditioning, propellants and blowing agents." It *is* more expensive than F-11 and F-12; but let nobody tell you that substitutes do not exist (that same report, by the way, ended with the note "other substitutes being considered include CFCs 142b and 152a, both of which are currently in production").

Alternatives that can be adequately used in the genuinely essential areas where CFCs have proved so useful (refrigeration in hospitals, for example, and cleaning computer circuitry) *already exist* and are being produced commercially. It would, in fact, be no more than a trivial economic hiccup for a few big businesses, something much less severe than the shakeup they all experienced in the stock market crash of 1987, if all nonessential uses of all of the dangerous CFCs were banned at once. And that would give the developed world a breathing space in which to convince developing countries (using the evidence of their own reaction to the problem) that there really is a threat to the global environment, and to offer them the alternative products. Why, Du Pont and ICI might even make money on the deal!

TOMORROW IS TOO LATE

Nor should anyone be deluded, anymore, into thinking that the problem of ozone depletion is one of increased risk of skin cancer for pale-skinned people. That is only a minor aspect of the story. I've already discussed the broad climatic and environmental implications. Even considering the Antarctic hole alone, biologists are now increasingly concerned at the hazard to phytoplankton posed by the increased ultraviolet reaching the ocean surface in the region. Sayed El-Sayed and colleagues from Texas A&M University have discovered that increased exposure to ultraviolet markedly decreases the activity of phytoplankton. But surely, I hear a voice saying, when you've seen one phytoplankton you've seen 'em all? Phytoplankton, in fact, form the base of the food chain on which fish, mollusks, and crustaceans depend. Who cares about the fish (and the penguins)? A timely analogy caught my eye in the *Guardian* on November 27, 1987.

By eradicating the tsetse fly, which causes sleeping sickness, African countries have opened up swampy regions to cultivation and to domesticated cattle. Wildlife immune to the disease—antelope, zebra, buffalo, and many more—are in retreat into shrinking regions, while their former territories are destroyed by overgrazing and sharp hooves, and are rapidly turning into deserts. "This is one of the most terrible things that has ever happened in Africa," said Raoul du Toit, of Zimbabwe's Department of Parks and Wildlife. A burgeoning disaster in the central core of Gaia, not out in the polar fringes, caused by the well-meaning effort to eradicate the tsetse fly. Nobody can predict the repercussions resulting from damage to Antarctic phytoplankton; but phytoplankton, at the base of the oceanic food chain, are far more important to Gaia than those flies.

The story of the hole in the sky, and its implications for humankind, is far from over. But it seems appropriate to close at least this phase of the story with comments from two of the leading participants. Joe Farman, who discovered the hole, wrote in his article in *New Scientist* on November 12, 1987, that "no one predicted these depletions. The lesson is plain: existing policies on the production of CFCs are based on a false premise—that we understand the processes controlling the ozone layer. The past few years have shown that we do not." And Sherry Rowland, in his talk at Chapel Hill on March 11, 1987, pointed out that "any agreement which affects only North America, Western Europe, and Japan will soon be overwhelmed by the increased usage outside these regions. If the goal is to prevent the organochlorine concentration of the atmosphere from growing much beyond that which has already produced the Antarctic ozone hole, then a phase-out of about 95 percent of existing uses will be required without *any* exceptions."

The Montreal agreement, even if it works, has committed us to an increase in stratospheric chlorine, Farman points out, to three times present levels by the year 2020—*ten* times the concentrations of chlorine present in the stratosphere before the use of CFCs became widespread. Even if by some miracle direct releases stopped immediately, Rowland concludes, ozone depletion would continue to increase for another two decades, because of the long lifetime of CFCs in the atmosphere. A lifetime of 120 years means that 90 percent of the CFC molecules already in the air in 1987 will still be there in 2000 A.D.; 39 percent will still be there in 2100 A.D.; and 7 percent even in 2300 A.D. The damage we have *already done* to the ozone layer will be with us, and our children and grandchildren, throughout the twenty-first and twenty-second centuries.

FURTHER READING

Several of my own books provide background on some of the topics touched on here. *Genesis* (New York: Delta; London: Oxford University Press) discusses the origin of life. *In Search of the Double Helix* (New York: Bantam; London: Corgi) deals with the detailed chemistry of life. *Future Weather* (New York: Delta; London: Pelican) looks into the greenhouse effect.

The definitive book about the ozone debates of the early to middle 1970s is *The Ozone War*, by Lydia Dotto and Harold Schiff (New York: Doubleday). Published in 1978, it goes into great detail on the political and scientific arguments about SSTs and spray cans in the United States; parts of chapters 2 and 3 of the present book draw on this source.

Georg Breuer's *Air in Danger* (New York: Cambridge University Press) and Louise Young's *Earth's Aura* (London: Allen Lane) deal in a more general way with global atmospheric pollution.

Jim Lovelock's definitive book *Gaia* is published by Oxford University Press, New York; a second Gaia book from Lovelock is due in 1988.

At a more technical level, several reports and conference proceedings volumes have appeared recently. The fruits of the Dahlem workshop on *The Changing Atmosphere* will be published in 1988. The UK Department of the Environment and the Meteorological Office published a joint report *Stratospheric Ozone* (available from HM Stationery Office) in 1987. The press release put out with this report was written without the approval of the authors and is not to be trusted (see chapter 8); the information in the report itself is sound. Friends of the Earth (London) published *Into the Void?*, a report on ozone depletion and CFCs by Kathy Johnston, in the same year, and the World Resources Institute (Washington, D.C.) published *The Sky Is the Limit*, by Alan Miller and Irving Mintzer, in 1986.

The most convenient place to find all of the chemical equations describing the reactions connected with stratospheric ozone depletion is in Sherry Rowland's booklet *Earth's Atmosphere in the Twenty-First Century*, published in 1987 by the University of North Carolina at Chapel Hill.

And as the debate about the impact of human activities on the ozone layer continues, the best place to keep up-to-date with new developments is in the pages of the weekly magazine *New Scientist*.

INDEX

ABOUT THE AUTHOR

JOHN GRIBBIN was born in 1946, in Maidstone, Kent, England. His Ph.D. in Astrophysics was awarded by the University of Cambridge in 1970, and after five years on the staff of the journal *Nature* and three with the Science Policy Research Unit at the University of Sussex, he became Physics Consultant to the weekly magazine *New Scientist* in 1978.

His previous book, *In Search of the Big Bang* completed a trilogy of major works on the most important scientific achievements of the twentieth century, which began with *In Search of Schrödinger's Cat* (1984) and continued with *In Search of the Double Helix* (1985). He also has co-written several science fiction novels. He contributes on science topics to the *Guardian* newspaper, as well as to *New Scientist*, and to the domestic and world services of BBC Radio.

He has won several awards for science writing, including the top British award, a Glaxo Travelling Fellowship, in 1974. Current projects include a collaboration with Mary Gribbin on the sociopsychology of being human, a science fiction novel, and a major book on the ultimate fate of the Universe, called *The Omega Point*.